# A CALL TO SERVICE

# A CALL TO SERVICE

*My Journey To The Ministry*

JOHN ELLINGTON

Paperback ISBN: 978-1-63337-445-4
E-book ISBN: 978-1-63337-446-1

LCCN: 2020919519

Printed in the United States of America

1 3 5 7 9 10 8 6 4 2

# CONTENTS

*I would like to dedicate this book to Mr. Ty Lawler. Many people have influenced and helped me along this walk, but this man has surpassed them all. Thank you for your instruction and guidance. Thank you for the work you have done within this ministry. Most of all, thank you for opening my eyes to the power of the Holy Ghost and enabling me to see God in a way I had never imagined. I have never encountered an individual who is more on fire for God than Brother Ty. Thank you, and we love you.*

# 1. The Beginning

I still live in the small rural community of Chatfield, Texas, where I have been since birth. As I always tell people, it's "about an hour south of Dallas." Once this was a wonderful, thriving place. Everyone knew everyone, and everyone helped each other. Fences and gates were present, but only to keep the livestock in, not us out. Slowly but surely, like all good things, this has come to an end. The community I was once so proud to be a part of has become filled with newcomers who mostly keep to themselves. Most community organizations are barely hanging on. We have a few of what I like to call socialites or posers: people who pretend to be good and to care about people and community but in truth couldn't care less. Most try to act as though they are a big part of things to impress others whom they think are important, yet when there is work to be done… they are absent.

Then there are those who have to constantly antagonize and berate those of us who are holding things together. I feel like they do it out of jealousy or maybe to try to make themselves feel important. I despise drama and, more so, those who create it. But, as God commands us, I do not return evil for evil. I continue to do good even for those who talk behind my back and the backs of others. I have found through my forty-year journey thus far that it is simply not worth my time to worry about them. What is important is this: God, wife and kids, family, those who need me, and finally, myself. Others may disagree with that order, but that is my list of priorities, and that is how I was raised.

Now this place isn't all that bad. There are still quite a few of us left with the "good ol' days" mentality. I have heard it said that one wasted time talking about or expecting those days to return. Instead, it was wiser to take the principles you learned from those days and introduce them to today. This is important because when your kids are grown, they will be referring to today as the "good ol' days." With that being said, don't waste time focusing on the past or what once was; instead focus on today, and build a future for tomorrow. So, a handful of us are trying to preserve our little community, and we are incorporating our children into that as well.

There is a lot to be said about the advantages of being raised in a small town such as this one. My parents took my brother, sister, and me to church every Sunday. After church, we met at my grandparents' house and had a Sunday dinner. Afterwards, the men would retire to the football game on TV, the women would remain around the table chatting, and us kids would be out in the pasture playing ball, army, chasing cows, or any other adventure that got our attention.

My entire family has been or still is involved in public safety professions. We all got our start in the local volunteer fire department (VFD), of which both of my grandfathers were charter members. Most of us still participate. There are a few posers who have infiltrated that organization too, but we still make it work despite that. Evenings meant a trip to the family lake for swimming or some local stock tank for fishing. Days meant hard work in which you better not complain. Community service was the focal point of my grandfather's work ethic. Believe me, he got his point across and instilled it in us kids as well. It stuck with most of us.

We cleaned the church each week. We worked a garden, divided the harvest, and delivered it to folks in town. We mowed grass and painted houses. We built fences and worked cows. We also had some down time and played as kids should. We spent many hours playing cards, forty-two, or Murder (a marble game my grandfather had made). In payment, we got to go fishing or swimming at the end of the day. Rarely did we get money, but when we did, we also received instructions on how to save it or spend it on something practical. My grandfather passed in December of 1995, and a part of all of us passed with him.

I have taken the values he instilled in me and have tried to live by them. I have also taken the values of my parents and my other grandfather and tried to mix them all together to make a good person. I think I have been pretty successful at that. There are those who would disagree with that, but frankly I don't care. I am out to impress God, my wife and kids, and that's about it. As long as God and myself know the truth, I'm good to go.

You should adopt the same attitude. It doesn't come overnight; it takes years. When you achieve it, truly achieve it, with a good heart and the right intentions, it makes life so much easier. Now, I don't mean to ignore everyone else, but you have to learn that you can't make everyone happy nor be responsible for all of their needs. You have to get your priorities straight. Some people will not be happy with you no matter what you say or do. Don't worry about that; it will give you unnecessary stress and make you die early, so let it go. Others will see your good heart and ride you like a jackass until you fall out. It's best to go ahead and buck them off early on. I know, easier said than done…I am still trying to figure that one out myself.

I grew up in what I did not know at the time was a rare thing. We had a happy, safe, pleasant home with both parents there and family nearby. I did well in school, all of us did, and had a really good childhood as far as I was concerned. I was not big into sports; as a matter of fact, I still could not care less. I liked to play baseball; although I was pretty good in our small town, I was pretty timid and didn't do as well on the Little League team. I still had fun, though. I focused mainly on the fire department, my livestock, and working during my school career. I didn't party much at all. There were a handful of us out here with similar backgrounds who hung out together. We mainly hunted, fished, camped, rode backroads, chased the riff-raff out of town, had the occasional brush pile to burn—you know (if you are lucky), good 'ol country boy stuff. I knew very little about drugs, dysfunctional families, getting into trouble, or even being grounded for that matter. There was no such thing as grounding in my day. It seems to have been a poor alternative as I look at a lot of today's society. I'm glad now that my parents didn't "spare the rod and spoil the child," so to speak.

It was, overall, a good childhood. I often wish I could relive it. I regret that I have not had the chance to provide that environment for my children, but I get as close as I can on the every-other-weekend basis that far too many fathers are familiar with today.

High school was a bore, mostly. The hardworking young man who pays his own way, serves his community, doesn't act a fool, and has his own things instead of Daddy's checking account and new truck wasn't very popular back in those days. Needless to say, I wasn't very popular, but I didn't care really. Again, I knew God was happy and I was doing the right thing, and I was okay with that. I was taking on adult responsibilities and seeing and doing things as a volunteer firefighter at a young age, and I was happy with that rather than being popular. I had earned the respect of grown men who ran into burning buildings for a living. I was good with that, and I placed a heck of a lot more value on that than on any sport. I guess we all turned out okay for the most part. Most of what I would call *normal* kids do the things I seem to speak negatively of during high school, but it just wasn't my thing.

By the time I graduated and was ready for college, I had a full-time job, a truck payment, a cell phone, and some livestock. I wanted to get a degree in electronics, but I had a small scholarship to the local junior college, so I had to go there. They really had nothing that caught my eye, but my love of the fire service had me wanting to be a fire marshal. So I enrolled in the criminal justice (CJ) program. It didn't take me long to figure out that college was just high school all over again. I found myself in a class full of kids with no direction who just wanted to party. I quickly found out I was better off attending the core CJ classes and working the rest of the time.

By my third semester, I was done with college. I seemed to be making it just fine without it. I was making money, making my own way. Probably overall a poor decision, but I was raised to be responsible and practical. I didn't think interviewing people at a basketball game to ask why they were there was a good use of my time. Nor was playing SimCity in sociology class for three months, nor reading a book and writing a paper on it. I was better off learning a trade and making money; it made a heck of a lot more sense to me at the time. Overall, I do not regret the decision.

Along the way, I was making quite the name for myself in the volunteer fire department world. At age eighteen, I was elected assistant chief of our department and I obtained my EMT-B certification. I attended every fire class that came up and was possible for me to go to. I rarely missed a call. I was and am proud to be a firefighter.

By the way, I made my first actual call when I was eight years old, and I haven't stopped yet.

I would like to thank all of those involved in raising me. I can't list every person here, but y'all were parents, teachers, church members, community members, and just overall great people. Of course, as always, there were some along the way from whom you learn what not to do. Too many children today sadly do not have the "raising" that we had, and for the most part, I think that is a bad thing. There was an even balance of work, fun, family, and education in my upbringing. I was fortunate to have several strong role models whom I respect and try to meet their mark still today.

Moving into the present day, I am pastoring a church that my wife and I started after much prayer and questioning. As I mentioned, I still live in the small rural community I was raised in. I am now the chief of the volunteer fire department, and I serve as the president of the board of the community center here, a historic building available for the public to rent as well as the hub for all community events. I have been divorced twice (more about that later), but I am currently married to a woman whom I firmly believe is the right one this time. I have four children ranging in age from nine months to sixteen years, two boys and two girls. My three oldest children I have not seen in quite some time due to the atrocity of family court, which is a national plague. The grandparents I spoke of are long since gone. I am blessed to be living in one of the home places of my childhood. I am a rock within the community in which several people depend on me for help on many projects. This is sometimes hard to handle, but all in all it is an honor to be the one they call upon because they know they can depend on me.

I have worked in all aspects of public safety. This is where I received a lot of my "training" for the call to ministry. I started as a child in our local volunteer fire department, and from there I moved on to a paid fire department. I also have family history in law enforcement and have served as a reserve officer and deputy sheriff, a paid officer and deputy sheriff, and a sergeant and chief of police in a small agency. I have also worked on an ambulance as both a paramedic and paramedic supervisor. I have many different certifications and have served as an instructor and field training officer in all three professions. To explain all of those experiences in complete detail will have to wait for another book. I have been involved in many life-and-death situations and have seen more than anyone should during those times, as have all who have walked in those shoes. I look at my current calling as the second phase of my life-saving career, as my health does not really allow me to walk in my former shoes anymore.

I have owned and operated many small service-oriented business, the latest being as a general contractor. My primary function was electrical contracting, which evolved into boat dock construction and repair. I have recently sold off the business, and my wife has gained employment as she wished to start a career. I now focus on our ministry and stay at home to handle small projects and to raise our daughter.

So, there you have the basic outline of my raising and current family situation. There are many, many things that could be discussed in greater detail, but that is not the purpose of this book. I am merely trying to give you a sample of my life and background ahead of the focus of the book, which is how I was called to ministry.

## 2. Marriage and Career

A s I mentioned in the previous chapter, I wasn't very popular in school. So, I imagine you can deduce from that statement that I wasn't all that popular with the ladies either. This definitely caused self-confidence issues, at least on the social side, some of which still affect the way I do things today.

I dated a young lady who was quite a bit younger than I was for a while during high school. Her mother and father knew my family and me; we went to church together. However, they weren't too happy with me dating their daughter because I was so much older. I can understand that now, but at the time it bothered me because I knew I was a good kid and that I didn't and wouldn't do anything to harm either of us. We are all friends today. I think the fact that I knew they didn't really want me there kind of rained on that parade, but everything happens for a reason, I guess.

So, there was this other young lady who lived up the road. When her family moved in, they were what we locals refer to as "implants" to our nice little town. I thought she was pretty, but I knew nothing at all about her. I was nineteen or twenty when we actually met. Her sister knew my cousin and they started coming to church, so it finally worked out that I could talk to her. One thing led to another, and we started dating. At the time, I thought, *Why is she with me?* Now I would say she was damn lucky to have me.

There were a ton of red flags during the relationship. She was at a party one night after ditching me, and let's just say she put on quite the show for some of those young punks out there. Of course, word got back to me immediately, and I was devastated. I was even more devastated when I called her after church and we ended it. I was mad as hell at her for doing that, and she lied to me, which hurt worse. After that, I would hear all kinds of things, and it still hurt.

Then, out of nowhere, here she came back, and here we go again. Love is blind I guess, and this was a first for me, so we were dating again. We were pretty steady for a little over a year when I started thinking, *Okay, it's time to get married now.* I thought it was right; it was what I saw all of my family and role models doing, so I thought this was the one.

After we were engaged, she came out one day without her ring and said, "Let's pretend we are not engaged for a while." I flipped out; the wedding was a couple of months away. That should have been the second clue, but nope, I was an idiot like many young men are. I shortly found out that her aunt, who had been married and divorced several times and at least twice more since we split, had been in her ear. I also found out that this aunt had bought her a one-way ticket to Spain. Needless to say, we didn't get along and still don't today.

My first wife had a strained relationship with her biological father. She claimed he didn't have much to do with her after her parents divorced. They all made him out to be a bad person. I met him; he always seemed nice and caring to me, but I wasn't there so I can't say for sure. So, since she had spent most of her time with her mother, she lacked a father figure, which explains her wild tendencies I mentioned earlier. It also explains her strained relationship with her stepfather who was a strict disciplinarian, in my opinion. Now, I don't agree with him on a lot of things—we had our differences—however, I can respect his opinion and his morals. She could not respect them, however, and quickly moved to her father's home. Once he tried to enforce some rules, she then ran to her grandparents' house. See the pattern yet?

In any event, we got married and moved into a brand new home I had bought right by the fire station in Chatfield. Now, this was a new mobile home that I financed for $48,000 sitting on about an acre of land that I had also bought. The place was nice. We made it a home with the dog and the whole nine yards. I fenced in the back half and built a barn that housed my chickens and her rabbits. We had a couple of sheep and cycled through a few calves.

She had a new vehicle and a part-time job. We pretty much did whatever she wanted to do. We were doing okay financially and took several small trips, had friends over, and had what seemed to be a pretty decent life going for our age.

At this time, I was working as an electrician. I was also attending several classes, meetings, training, and responding to emergency calls. I was president of the county fire association as well. I was basically building my résumé and working my way into public safety. I eventually went to work for the fire department full time, as well as becoming a reserve police officer at a local small-town police department. All of this was done in an effort to improve our financial standing and stability and to advance my career, which in turn would be better for the family. She, however, made the statement that I was doing all of this to "get my name in the paper." I didn't then and still don't care about publicity for my accomplishments. It does, however, bother me when someone else takes credit for my work publicly— but that is another story.

We began to argue more often. She seemed to want to draw a line in the sand between herself and the rest of my family and career. I found a diary in which she was writing about being unhappy and the unrealistic idea of riding off into the sunset with a cowboy on the beach. This most likely stemmed from all of the romance novels she had started reading. She also had some socialite family in her ear trying to talk her into leaving me. Her people never thought I was good enough for them. I didn't really think a lot about it; I figured it was pretty much just daydreaming. All in all, I thought we got along just fine.

About this time, we discovered that we were pregnant with our daughter, my first child. It was also about this time that I noticed she had a small suitcase packed under the bed. I guess she was about to make riding off into the sunset a reality right before she found out we were going to have a child. Needless to say, her people were less than excited about the baby, though all of my side were very excited.

The pregnancy seemed to straighten her out for a while. We were happy again and everything seemed to be good again. I thought that maybe this was going to fill the void she felt and all would straighten out, but I was wrong. Before my daughter's first birthday, she was standing at the door, baby and suitcase in hand, ready to leave. So, she left to her parents' house that night with my daughter. I was beside myself; this was not supposed to happen. I was lost, embarrassed, and did not know what to do.

The next day, I was supposed to go on shift at the fire department for twenty-four hours. I went to work and acted as if everything was fine. When I returned home the next morning, my house was empty. She and her family had come and cleaned it out while I was at work.

A short time later, all of the finance companies started calling as all of the bills were three months behind. So began the demise of my financial status that would last for the next several years.

The most important thing that was lost was time with my daughter. Yes, my pride, heart, reputation, social standing, my faith, et cetera, all took a huge hit, but someone taking your child away is terrible beyond imagination. The fact that the cards are stacked against the father in family court is absolutely disgusting. They dictate what you can and can't do with your own flesh and blood, tax your finances to the point that you can barely survive, much less do much for your children, and as a father, there is absolutely nothing you can do to change it. It is a very sad situation, and it plagues fathers all across this nation. Despite this drastic tragedy, my daughter and I maintained a good relationship up to the weekend of her thirteenth birthday, which we will discuss later.

I moved my career forward and switched from the fire department to the police department in another city. I worked there as a reserve officer and occupied my time risking my life for free when I was off from my paying job, just to give me something to do. They made me feel valuable and appreciated, which was something severely lacking in all other aspects of my life at the time. When I made the switch, several people warned me and were surprised about my decision, but they didn't know the battles I was fighting and why I needed this change.

Eventually, I made chief of that department, and just as I had been warned about, the corruption of small-town politics infiltrated my position a short five years later. I was and am a man of moral standards and integrity, and I refused to bow down to corruption, so I took the fight to them. In the end, I learned that people I once called friends, and others in positions of authority whom I had respected, were not who I thought they were. I found out that one, either they lacked backbone, or two, they had just been lying and putting up a false front the whole time I knew them. I resigned from the career position that I thought was going to dictate my future and legacy. I was already working a second full-time job at that point for an EMS agency, which made me a supervisor only seven months into my employment there.

After being divorced for the first time, a couple of years later I met someone else. She was the daughter of my boss at the police department. We were all close and hung out together a lot. I ended up dating and eventually marrying her. Everything was going well: we had the house, careers, family, and eventually two children, both boys. Eventually we started fighting a lot; her mother and I had a strong difference of opinion across the board, which was the beginning of the demise. My boys were three and four years old at the time of the divorce. The divorce was nasty, and she still torments me to this day. I lost my home, my vehicles, everything—and most important, I now had lost two more children and was paying even more child support. This led me to be a grown man, father of three, dirt poor and living with my parents again. My children and I still made the best of our relationship and our time together. We were all hurt and sad, but we made the best of it.

The second wife is one of the most drama-inspired, wicked people I have encountered. She was and still is constantly talking me down in public, to my children and doing any and everything possible to make my life a living hell. This led to many, many court appearances, financial problems, the loss of careers and professional licenses, and eventually an eighteen-day stay in the local cross-bar motel, which I'll address later in this book.

It was during this time in my life when I began to question my faith. This was a period when I wasn't necessarily separated from God—I still believed—but I was extremely mad at Him. I was beginning to think I had wasted my time serving others, giving of myself, sacrificing, praying, being nice, and all that dictates what most consider to be the qualities of a good Christian person. I secluded myself, drank a lot, stayed mad, didn't eat, and gave up on most of my service projects and positions. I was just in a dark place in my life. I had lost all respect for myself and all that I stood for, all that I had worked for and believed in, and probably the worst of all was that I had lost respect for God. I straightened up and held it together for my kids when they were there, but once they were gone back to their mothers' places, I went back to the dumps.

During this period, I was working as a paramedic supervisor full time and as a firefighter part time, and still was the assistant chief of our local VFD. I also did some side jobs contracting. I pretty much burned the candle at both ends with little to eat, very little sleep, and little downtime. Other than the weekends when I had my children, I was in the pasture cutting trees, burning brush, drinking, and staying secluded. I felt as if I had no friends; I was embarrassed by the state my life was in, and I stopped helping others because I felt as if I was a failure. Again, I believed in God, but I was very mad. I always asked Him, "Why are You punishing me? I lived to serve and do good for others even at expense to myself! Have I not been good enough? Have I wasted all of these years?"

As you can tell, it was dark, and I was broken. I didn't know it at the time, but didn't Job have a similar situation? Didn't Job actually suffer more than I was suffering? The difference between Job and me was that he never lost faith; Job stood strong. Even when his friends were doubting God and his wife tried to encourage him to take his own life, Job stayed the course.

I continued on in my career path, earning the respect of my co-workers and others in the profession. I received several awards and commendations. I was really good at what I did, but I was dead inside. I had very little self-respect and felt unworthy of anything. I knew every aspect of my job backward and forward, and I was respected by many in my field. I trained others, served on boards and committees, wrote standards, and even wrote several classes in which people actually paid to come hear me talk—which I thought was unheard of. I have written several letters and presented several ideas and protocols for which others have taken credit and used. It always amazed me that I could read my work in the local newspaper and see and hear people quoting my words as if they were their own. In the end, I didn't really make a fuss over it because usually it worked out for the greater good. I often feel as though this is one reason, outside of my three years as chief of police, why I never was given a rank or promotion at my paying jobs in public safety. I personally feel, and have been told by many others, that I was very good at what I did and intelligent to the point that I was intimidating. Therefore, the powers that be wanted to keep me suppressed, keep me in the shadows and use my ideas to keep me from taking their jobs. This is a bold and arrogant statement for me to make, and one that is contradictory to my true feelings. This was especially true at that time, as I didn't expect anything or credit for my work, just respect and acceptance. I was not after anyone's job. All of my actions and ideas were meant to be for the greater good, not for individual recognition.

I also didn't play politics well. I called a snake a snake, I didn't buy into cliques of financial power. My lips, pride, morals, and upbringing have a huge dislike for the taste of other people's rear ends. If there was a problem with procedure, I pointed it out and offered a solution. If there was a person in charge who shouldn't be, I pointed it out. This was not for self-gratification or advancement; it was meant to fix a broken system to protect the public. After all, we weren't building televisions here, where if one failed no one was hurt. We were dealing with lives and property, working in a field where if a problem wasn't addressed, someone could potentially die! It all made sense to me, but as we all know, in this day and age, status, finances, and political connections are usually the driving force behind most things.

I left my paying jobs at both the fire department and the EMS company and moved my career back home to the local sheriff's office. Once again, I thought this was where I would serve out the rest of my public safety career. Once again, God had other plans. I truly enjoyed my time spent there, and I enjoyed police work. The usual politics and disappointments were there just like anywhere else, but the good outweighed the bad, and overall, I was happy. I soon found myself sleeping while my kids were around as I worked deep nights. I was losing time with them, which is more valuable than anything. I realized that my kids had not spent the night in their room at my house in almost a year, as they went to my parents' on nights I had to work. My contracting jobs began to pick up and I had always dreamed of running my own business, so once again, I made a career change. I ran my own company for the next five years, and today I run a church. Many things change, and our plans are futile. Only God knows what He has in store for us.

Now, during the career paths I mentioned above, there were good times, but I was still dead inside. I felt alone, my self-worth was in the dumps, and I didn't see many people. I dated a couple of women, which turned out to be a mistake. I made some dumb decisions that I think were mainly based on my lack of faith at the time, my opinion of myself, and just out of a pure feeling of worthlessness and being lonely. I put up with stuff that I wouldn't even think about living through today. Looking back, the main thing missing was God. I had lost faith, I didn't turn to Him, I was mad at Him, and I couldn't understand why He was punishing me. It seemed that every time I turned around, there He was, punching me in the gut again. I had no home of my own, no money, a crappy vehicle, no real friends, limited time with my children, my knowledge and ideas had been stolen, I had basically no fun times at all (except with my children), and I was basically just the exterior shell of a man running on autopilot and energy drinks.

I'll let you in on a little something I knew nothing about at the time but that makes perfect sense now:

**James 1:2-4 (NLT) Dear Brothers and Sisters, when troubles of any kind come your way, consider it an opportunity for great joy. For you know that when your faith is tested, your endurance has a chance to grow. So let it grow, for when your endurance is fully developed, you will be perfect and complete, needing nothing.**

So, I was being tested. I must have just barely passed that test. That is my opinion, at least. I believed that God was there, but at this point in my life that is where it ended. I prayed empty prayers, not expecting an answer; if I did get an answer, it seemed as if it was always the opposite of what I thought I needed. I didn't let Him take over as I should have. Yet He was always there, training and molding me, which I did not see at the time, but I saw it when it was His time and for His purposes. I wish I had been closer with God at the time and had been in my Bible, but I wasn't. I credit that to being raised in a religious box, as I call it: the local Methodist church.

Don't get me wrong here. (Someone is already highlighting that sentence to try to use it against me.) I am not knocking the local church congregation. I was raised in and had a big part in that church for quite some time. Sometimes I was more active than others, but haven't we all been guilty of being idle at times? I did not realize at the time the true power of God and Scripture. I credit this to the "Method" in Methodist. We came in on Sunday, said the same words, sang a couple songs, listened to a sermon, said some more words, and went home. The impact just wasn't there, or at least not for me, as I now know. Therefore, I wasn't buried in the Bible as I should have been. I didn't know God's words.

Sure, I believed, I knew some of the stories, but I never saw or realized the true power of God. God was not the center; the man-made doctrine and routine was. In most churches I have been to (until lately), if someone spoke of God working in his or her life, that person was seen as a fanatic or senseless. "God don't just take care of you. You have to do something yourself," I would hear. People, I now know that God does move, God will take care of you, and even your darkest day has a divine purpose. (See the Scripture from the book of James again.)

Before I get going on church and God showing up in my life, I need to finish explaining what my professional career path actually entailed for those who don't know the job. A few of you will have already put the pieces together, but most will not have. I was what was known as being triple certified, sometimes referred to as a public safety officer. This is someone who has achieved certification as a firefighter, paramedic, and peace officer. I was also a certified instructor in all three fields. I achieved many other certifications and underwent many, many hours of additional training in all three fields. I have seen people at their best, but mostly at their worst. Death and I have met more times than I care to describe. There are images in my head of dead children, babies, adults, senseless acts of violence, torn families, ruined lives, scarred loved ones, and the list goes on. I have been cussed at, spit at, shot at, berated, disrespected, and at times ashamed of what I had to do. I have lost count of the number of times I have told people their loved ones were dead despite our efforts, lost count of the CPR saves—unlike on television, the deaths highly outnumber the saves. I have cried, I have blamed myself, my life is lived on high alert—watching people, doors, planning escape, planning for the worse. That isn't on duty; that is every second of every day, in a restaurant, store, highway. Anywhere we go, my head is on a swivel.

Why, you may ask? Because I have seen what happens when you don't stay on alert. This is something I try to move past but find impossible to do; I have seen too much. This is a noble calling and profession and takes a strong person to take any one of these jobs on, much less all three at once. Most importantly, it takes God in your life to help you along the way. Give it to Him. I used to tell people I have encountered in the medical field that living and dying is not up to us, it is up to God. Don't take it personally; be grateful that God gave you a talent and put you in that place at that time so He could work through your hands and give comforting words through your mouth. That in itself is one of the highest honors you will ever have: being the hands of God, doing His work.

# 3. God Shows Up

So now that you know a little about my background as far as my childhood, family situation, and previous career paths, it is time to get to the meat and potatoes of the thing, which is how God showed back up in my life and led me to ministry. Plenty of people out there will be glad to tell you that I am not qualified for ministry, especially after they read that last chapter. If you are exploring your calling, some like them have probably told you the same thing. Do not let them discourage you. Only you know what God is telling you, and it is not for them to decide. It is strictly between you and God.

I finally began to realize that something had to give. I was headed to an early death. Working constantly, staying angry, being lonely, no sleep are all very stressful things and take a toll on your body. Later on, I developed high blood pressure, chest pains, and I believe a little touch of congestive heart failure (CHF). This is what going at it alone will get you. You have to let God step in; He is sitting right there beside you waiting on you to call upon Him.

**Romans 10:13 (NLT) For everyone who calls on the name of the Lord will be saved.**

I began to give in a little. Bad things were still happening, but my heart was beginning to soften again. I asked myself, "Why are you mad at God? He is all powerful, you have been told this your whole life. Something is going on and you have to figure it out. He is still the gatekeeper to Heaven." I knew that even though I did not understand and I was mad, God could not be ignored. I began to pray more for help, but I still did not expect any answers.

Then He began to show out in my life. It seemed that everyone I picked up in the ambulance wanted to talk about God. Everyone was quoting Scriptures. I could not drive one hundred yards without seeing a billboard about God or a Scripture. It was always numbers, never the actual words. At the time, I did not have a Bible handy; I had no idea where mine was at. It never dawned on me to look the Scriptures up on the internet or my phone. Today I use them all the time. Although God did not reveal that option to me until much later, it was still part of His plan. I went to a local chain store one day to get a Bible, thinking they would be cheap, but surprisingly, I could not afford it, which only angered me more. I did not know then that still, He had a couple more things to show me before He put a Bible in my hand.

One Saturday I was on duty at the fire department. It was someone's birthday, and we were usually slow on the weekends, so I had a couple racks of ribs on the smoker for dinner. I have a pretty decent reputation on the smoker, by the way. I stepped outside to check on things, and while I was out there, a man walked up and started talking to me. He talked for ten minutes or so about how much he enjoyed barbeque and how his son cooked and was having a birthday party out of town the next day. This gentleman was maybe in his late sixties. We were just carrying on talking, and all of a sudden, he said, "Well, the reason I came up here is because I think I'm having a heart attack."

I about fell over and asked why didn't he say something, and then I summoned the rest of the crew. I helped him into the ambulance as I was the lead medic that day. He told me that he'd had chest pains the previous night, and he basically went on to describe all of the symptoms of having a heart attack. At the time he was with me, he really had no complaints medically. I placed him on the cardiac monitor, and let's just say the rhythm was scary. He said he had not had a heart attack previously, but the monitor was saying, in layman's terms, that we needed to be at the hospital five minutes ago. I was in a quandary, because he had described having a heart attack the night before, the monitor was screaming at me, but my patient basically had no symptoms. I contacted medical control, and they were as confused as I was. So, we transported him to the hospital.

During the ride in, this man began to ask me about my life. I gave the standard answer: everything was peachy. But he stated to me in no uncertain terms that he knew it was not. He then went on to briefly describe that I was getting no rest, had doubts, and was questioning my faith. Being surprised yet again, I began to give the outline of where I was physically and spiritually. He kept saying, "Proverbs three, five and six." Obviously I knew this was Scripture, but I asked him what it was, and he just repeated it again. I knew this was strange, but I also knew that these things could only be the work of God, although I had never knowingly witnessed such a thing and had been told that this type of stuff did not happen anymore. The man remained calm, spoke about how God works and how He does not forsake us, and kept saying, "Proverbs three, five and six," and told me to look it up. I dropped him off at the

ER and went on about my routine, still pretty much amazed at what had just happened.

After this, my eyes were really open, and I began watching. Later on that evening, here he comes again. He said he was released from the ER and all was well, and that he had returned to retrieve his vehicle. He asked if I had looked at the Scripture yet. I said no, as I didn't have a Bible with me. He just nodded his head and began to talk about barbeque again. By now the ribs were done, so I gave him a couple. He asked what time I got off work, and I told him at 7:00 a.m. the next day. He then told me he went to the church near the station and that I should come by there the next morning. I told him that I might do that. I think we both knew that I would not, but he said, "Okay then, I'll be waiting for you." I saw this as just nice talk and didn't think anything else of it. He then left and went on about his day, as did I.

As I mentioned earlier, my vehicle was not the best in the world, so on that particular Saturday, I'd had someone drop me off at work and they were supposed to pick me up the next morning. Well, in true fashion, I was let down again. Seven o'clock came and my ride was not there. Seven thirty came, and still, my ride wasn't there. I called multiple times on the phone and got no answer. Long story short, they finally showed up at 10:00 a.m. I was angry, to say the least. As we were driving away, we passed the church the man had spoken of. I kid you not, there he was sitting in a chair by the front door. As we drove by, he waved at me and began to get up to leave. If the last twenty-four hours had not been interesting enough, I guess God was going to show up this day too. I realized that while I had been sitting there angry, God had made a way for me to go to church with that man. But I didn't listen. The man did not know me, yet he waved as I went by. He knew it was me, and when I passed, he got up because he saw that I was not coming.

I have yet to see him again. Explain to me again, folks, how God is not present on this Earth and how He is not trying to get our attention. I'll wait.

The next shift was no different: Scripture everywhere I looked. I had also been picturing in my head my children and me sitting in a place with trees and me reading from the Bible to them. We like to camp and be outdoors, so I had it in my mind that I would get a small Bible with a sleeve so that it would easily fit into a backpack and be protected. When we made our morning run to the grocery store to get food for the day, I was bound and determined to get a Bible. I found it, the very Bible I was reading to my kids from, small, with a sleeve, perfect. I looked at the price tag. It had been marked down from twelve dollars to $9.97. Bibles have no tax and I only had ten dollars to my name. I bought the Bible and before we got back to the station I read the Scripture:

**Proverbs 3:5-6 (NLT) Trust in the Lord with all your heart; do not depend on your own understanding. Seek his will in all you do, and he will show you which path to take.**

God was calling. He had been calling for a couple years now. He sent people to me, He showed me Scripture. Finally, He sent a man to talk to me directly, because I'm pretty hard-headed, evidently. So, I read Proverbs and at that point I gave in. I prayed to God then and there. I said, "I see You, but I do not know what You want of me." I asked for guidance. I spent the next several minutes thumbing through the Bible, reading a word here and there, not really knowing what to do.

Then, the words of my earthly father rang in my head. A while back we had been having a conversation about my situation and he said something that contained the line, "Look at Job." Those words came into my mind, and I immediately began to read the book of Job. I was amazed: I was Job. Now, Job had it worse than I did, but I can seriously relate to him. It took me several days to read the book of Job, and I can honestly say I was amazed at what I was reading. It was me.

I finished Job, and as soon as I did, I realized I wasn't done. I had a strong desire to keep reading, but I again did not know where to go next. I kept picturing reading to my kids. I went back to Proverbs and began reading. I soon realized that this was a book of wisdom, much like a father passing valuable words of life to his children, just like I had pictured in my head over and over. As I continued to read this book, I realized that it contained many of the principles that were taught to me as a child. I saw many things stated where I realized I had strayed and taken the wrong path. I also soon realized, looking back to my time with Job to now, that while I was reading the Bible, the world seemed to stand still. My phone did not ring, tones did not drop at the station, time seemed to stand still, and I realized I had a feeling of extreme peace. I also realized that when I stopped reading, things picked back up and became hectic again. All of this was a new experience for me, and I was in awe. I had no idea how much more God would do with me and what I was in for.

I didn't know who to tell about this. I knew God was talking to me in a most direct and visible way, but who would believe me? Most people I knew would say, "Yep, he finally lost it." I had to tell someone. I had questions; I needed someone to tell me this was real and not my imagination. I went to the most loving Christian woman I have known, my grandmother.

I have to take a minute to tell you about her. Her faith was strong. She believed that God was ever present and working in our lives every day. She knew Scripture and she knew how we were to live, and she did her best to hold us accountable to that effect. She always told me how much she thought of me and how proud she was of me. She told me that she was proud of how strong I was and that I had not given up despite life's challenges. I told her it was hard, but I was hanging in there. I couldn't bear to tell her how I really felt inside, but she was right, I had hung on and now was seeing the light again. She always told me she prayed for the enemies every night, just as God tells us to. She said, "It sure is hard, but I do it every night." She answered the few questions I had, mainly reassuring me that what I was seeing, feeling, and hearing was real. She told me to keep it up. She checked in with me several times during this transition and was always really interested in what was happening now.

I worked my way through Proverbs, and after a few weeks, I was almost at the end. It was just about time to leave to go pick the kids up from school. I remember thinking, *I may have just enough time to finish these last few pages.* I was reading, and again, time seemed to stand still. I finished the book and still had time to spare. I remember thinking out loud, "Okay, what do I read next?" But the answer did not come. I tried to think about it, but it just didn't happen. So again, I thumbed through the pages and I came to the section titled "How to Read the Bible." Well, that didn't interest me much, and I also did not have much time to read, so I thumbed again. My finger stopped on a page, and I read a line that went something like this: "Do not let time be a measure by which you read the Bible." Again, I was in awe. I figured it was time to put it away and think about all of this.

On my drive to the school, I reflected on the signs with Scripture, the man who had met me at the station, what I had read in the book, and I made what I guess you would say is a promise to myself. I said, *From now on, I am going to look at things differently. I am going to be at peace, I am going to be slow to anger, and I am going to trust more in God.*

Almost at that very moment, God said, "Okay, let's find out." My phone started ringing again with people I really did not want to deal with or talk to. I got to the school and my kids were not there. It was my day. I found myself angry. I called their mother, and naturally she began with her smart mouth and her harassing talk. As it turned out, I didn't respond quite as nicely as God would have wanted. There had been a simple mistake; supposedly, the other grandparents had picked them up. Now our plans were altered and my time was lost. *How dare they?* I thought. My anger consumed me.

Finally, a couple hours later, my boys were with me and all was right with the world again, except for one thing. I realized that I had said I would change and be at peace, and immediately I was tested and failed. The difference was that this time I took notice. This time I had hope because I *knew* God was with me and watching me. I knew God was doing something with me, even though I had no idea what it was or where it would go. For the first time in a long time, I had hope again.

I kept that Bible with me everywhere I went. Each time I saw a Scripture, I looked it up. Nothing really astounding came to me. I couldn't place any particular meaning to what I was seeing. Looking back now, I was just being filled and staying in the Word. I started taking note of things. I found what bothered me, and I began to pause and make the conscious choice not to let things bother me. I began to trust God again. People came to me asking where Bibles were in the store. People on the ambulance continued to talk Scripture with me, and this time I had more to say because I had a renewed fire for God. I did not really know what was going on, but now I listened more intently when they spoke. Then it just kind of faded away.

God wasn't speaking to me anymore. I have had a voice in my head since childhood that I know is Him: not a doubt in my mind. I still have it today. Many people do, as I have found out. I was still realizing things and growing, but it just wasn't slapping me in the face anymore. I tried to read the Bible but couldn't get interested. Looking back, I'm guessing that He touched me and then gave me another test for a couple years to see what I was going to do with it. I continued to pray. I saw some things come to light and others that did not. I prayed for guidance and protection and for the health and happiness of my children. I thanked Him daily. I wasn't praying a profound prayer by any means. It was simple, generic, and pretty much the same night after night. All in all, my outlook had changed quite a bit, and I was getting better.

As I sit here and reflect while writing this, I am in a much better frame of mind. I am much happier and have grown tremendously in my spiritual life. I realize that God doesn't get in much of a hurry to do anything most of the time. After all, He waited on me to come knocking for at least two years. He then spent a few months walking with me in a manner that made His presence very much known and clear to me, and then He kind of faded away. I knew He was there, but I yearned for that presence I had once felt; I wanted it back. It came back in due time, but I believe He gave me two more years to work on what I had learned and to grow and improve.

# 4.  The Next Test

J umping forward to the end of the two-year stretch where God
was there—just not as vocal, I might say—I had made the transition from the public safety world into self-employment. Things were
going okay; not great, but okay. I was getting out more, I was trusting God, and my business was keeping the bills paid. I was, however,
falling behind on child support. This happened for two reasons: one,
it is almost impossible to get a person at the attorney general's office,
child support division, on the phone. I simply did not know how to
pay it, and there was no one to tell me. The second was that it really
got under my skin to be paying an absurd amount of money to those
who sought to destroy me. I knew that most of it was not going
toward my children, so I did not make it a priority. Say what you will
about it; my kids were happy and taken care of in both homes, mine
and hers.

I was finding myself surrounded by people who seemed to care
about me. Later on, I felt I was being led down the wrong road and
that I was more like a court jester than part of the crowd. Later this
was confirmed to me. My kids were beginning to say they wanted
more time with me, and even that they wanted to live with me. I
knew this would be next to impossible to accomplish. They were
torn; they wanted us both equally, not just four or six days per month

with Dad. Any decent human, much less a loving parent, should be able to understand that concept. You would think the courts, who supposedly stand for justice, would think the same thing. For the most part, you would be wrong on both counts. I really study and research this; it is an epidemic, it is atrocious, and I cannot believe that it is allowed to remain this way. This will come into play later.

I began to talk with my kids, mainly my two boys, about the possibility of 50/50 time with each of us. I thought it would take a miracle to make this happen, but it was the only thing I thought would be remotely possible. As I was thinking this out and working through options, suddenly I got served with child support papers. I figured this was as good a time as any to address the atrocious amount of money I was being charged, as well as to seek a custody change. After all, I was being billed for child support based on about $35,000 more per year than I was actually making and had been for years.

Just a side note, I was told that I had the "potential" to make that amount of money, so that was what I would be charged for. I told them I also had the potential to win the Powerball too; did they just want to go ahead and charge me like I had millions? One makes just about as much sense as the other. I can't give it to you if I don't have it, yet I am held accountable for not giving what I don't have. Go figure.

This turned into the battle of a lifetime, and I am still fighting it today. As I write this, I have not seen my three older children in four years. This time, I kept my faith. This time, I handled the test differently in even worse conditions. I will try to sum up the family court situation as briefly as I can, as it is not the point of this book. I will say that this is a sickness that must be fixed; it is very near and dear to my heart. I could write another book about my experience in the family court system and all that is wrong with it and will one day most likely.

I went to a lawyer based on the advice of what I thought was someone who cared. I paid money to this person and she was rude and short with me the whole time. I offered to make a down payment on the retainer that day and have the rest in a couple weeks, but she refused. When I did get the full retainer, she stated that I could not hire her as she had been retained by my ex-wife. There is absolutely *no* way that I will *ever* be convinced that she had not already been hired by the ex when I went in and spoke with her, gave her my evidence, told her my plan, turned over my whole case to her to review and advise me on—after which she kept all the documents. I had unknowingly just handed my last straw, my battle plan, into the hands of the enemy. I immediately filed a complaint with the state bar association and hired another lawyer. He assured me that everything would be fine when I paid him $4,750. He did nothing. His court appearances were a joke. He let them run all over me and said nothing. During this process, my kids were taken away from me; I was not allowed to see them over a completely false accusation.

How do I know this was a false accusation, you may ask? Here is how: I was investigated by law enforcement, and they said no offense occurred. A trained professional interviewer was called in, and they said not only was it unfounded, but one of the children had been coached on what to say. In my law enforcement career, that was a red flag that would get a case thrown out, but not here; the devil and his advocates were at work. Child Protective Services (CPS) was then called. Their representatives came and talked to all involved—all attorneys—came and inspected my home, and said all was well and the accusations unfounded.

So how did they accomplish this? When the first three attempts failed, they went to the district judge in family court, told him the same story and he just blindly signed an order and barred me from seeing my kids. I was never asked a question, never given my chance in court, nothing. That, my friends, is pure injustice that rips families apart, hurts children, and leads to violence and suicide among torn fathers. It also leads children to depression, social problems, drugs, anger, and many other issues. Why? It is the devil himself attacking us at the core of the family and using man's law to perpetuate it. Throughout all the court appearances I was always brought up to the stand, and the opposing lawyer ripped into me, trying to destroy my credibility, reputation, fatherhood—you name it, she attacked it.

I was in the presence of a CPS employee, a peace officer, a captain in the fire department, an ER nurse, and a deputy chief of a large EMS company on the night of the supposed incident. Did they ever get to testify? Of course not. Each time it was finally my turn to get someone on the stand, the judge magically had to be somewhere else. He would suspend the trial and the next time it picked up, did it start with my side calling witnesses? Nope, it was back to the woman berating me with lies on the stand again. If I denied it, or produced documentation proving the point, it was ruled hearsay. I did finally get one witness on the stand for a grand total of forty-one seconds. Although the lawyers and judge were screaming and yelling and basically wasted the whole time, the witness did say that I was a good father.

There are two more observations, out of several I have made during this process, that I would like to mention here. The opposing lawyer was drunk in a restaurant and was having a very easy conversation with my so-called friends, trashing me and stating that the judge was going to do this and that, *before the court date was set.*

The judge did just as she said he would do. It makes you wonder. I also have pictures of my so-called friends communicating with the opposing attorney, whom they agreed was evil in front of me, and also of all of the lawyers who supposedly worked for me, or claimed to be my friends, or to support my cause, all sitting in each other's laps and having drinks, as well as text messages between all of them.

So, the point of this is: be careful who you trust, because serpents stick together and are very smart and cunning. If you stand back and watch, you will observe that evil congregates just as Christians do. God tells us to turn the other cheek, that vengeance is His and to let Him have it. Trust me, it has been very hard to do all of those things, but I have. I have also seen Him at work. I know He is not finished yet and He is using this for His divine purpose. My faith has made me strong!

> **Habakkuk 1:4 (NLT) The law has become paralyzed, and there is no justice in the courts. The wicked far outnumber the righteous, so that justice has become perverted.**

> **John 16:33 (NLT) I have told you all this so that you may have peace in me. Here on Earth you will have many trials and sorrows. But take heart, because I have overcome the world.**

Through all of this, I will not pretend that I did not get angry and let some bad thoughts run through my head, but overall, I feel I have handled this well on a spiritual level. I see it as another test, another example that God is showing me this world. He is testing and educating me; He has allowed me to be dragged through a bad scenario. However, my faith is stronger this time; I have believed in and stuck by Him instead of becoming angry and resentful. I have learned some things, and I have seen the true person behind those who pretended to be for me. He has shown me this terrible thing and has molded me in the fire of it, and He has made me stronger so that I may stand and fight and help others who are walking the same path. I get it, and I am actually happy about being dragged through the fire. It has strengthened me spiritually and mentally. I won't tell you I am not hurt, that I don't cry often, and even that I don't get angry on occasion. I also feel a little guilty for having happy moments without them. I think of my kids daily. I know that God is in control and that He is using this evil work to make me, my family, and my children stronger.

Even as all of this was happening, I was still working and making it okay in that regard. I was living life, but found once again that I could easily slip off the edge and be back in depression, anger, hopelessness, et cetera. The difference was that this time I was not angry with God. I was reading books, observing God's presence, and in my Bible. I still wasn't very strong with my Bible yet, but at least I had it.

You must also understand that several things were happening simultaneously during this time. While family court was ripping my life apart, my business was somewhat thriving. I did not renew any of my public safety certifications, as I was afraid they might be stripped during this court process. I did not want my legacy and accomplishments to be taken on their terms, so I let them expire, on my terms. This process took a couple of years to play out in court. I will admit that I was pretty upset during all of this, but again, God was at work. I did not see it so much at the time, but He became present again.

I again became embarrassed with the situation. Once again I was being dragged through the mud, and my reputation as a good Christian man, a father, and a good public servant was under attack. Many people whom I had known my whole life and who knew of my accomplishments and good works were now talking bad about me.

When they saw me they would turn away and avoid speaking to me. Since then I have developed a new understanding through walking closer with Christ, and that understanding is that it doesn't matter what the world calls you; it only matters that Jesus calls you. Through everything that has happened, and all of those people who condemn me because they don't know the whole story, I know that Christ loves me and approves of me. Otherwise, why would He be blessing me in so many ways and making His presence in my life known?

Just about the time I started feeling pretty much destroyed and useless, God sent me someone who was seeking my advice. Victoria, a young lady whom I had known for quite some time, sought me out for advice on entering the public safety field. She knew me and the family and our long, solid history in this profession. Later, she told me that she had a dream in which God told her to come find me. She did just that. She decided to enter the medical field and enrolled in EMT basic training.

During this course, we began to meet at our local fire station, of which I served as chief at this point, to train on what she was learning. A strong friendship quickly developed. Through several months of this, her life too began to become unraveled with family issues, living arrangements, and transportation. Even though I was deep in struggle myself, I saw an opportunity to help someone. I allowed her to move into my house, which had two bedrooms; she was in one and I mostly stayed in the living room. We arranged for her to have transportation and a place to stay. In return, she did the books for my business, helped around the house, and did my advertising.

We quickly decided that we needed each other in our lives. What started out as me helping someone, which may be hard for some to believe since it was a male and female in the same house, turned into something huge. We are now happily married, have a daughter, and another child on the way. During our time together, we have helped each other develop spiritually and professionally. She graduated as valedictorian of her EMT class. I was getting stronger in the Bible and was feeling like I needed to enter the ministry. I felt a strong pull in that direction, and she was very encouraging. At first, I felt like it was a mistake; I felt that due to my past I wouldn't be accepted. I fought it for a long time, but the pull got stronger.

Soon we established an office location in town, and the business really took off. I had four employees and things were going well. The bills were paid, and I thought finances were going to be okay now. Yet I kept feeling the call to ministry. I taught public safety training regularly, and I really enjoyed talking to people and teaching. I had seen a lot of things in my career, and I felt that I was pretty good at helping people by talking to them. I thought, *What better way to help someone than to lead them to Christ?* I still pushed back with a feeling of inadequacy.

Finally, one night our local church was having a revival. Victoria and I were in attendance, and a man was preaching, talking about his call to ministry. He said, "I can lead, build, and teach. Isn't that what church is?" He was referring to his past work in which he led men, he built things, and he taught others. He was exactly right, too. You lead people in an organization, build it up, and teach the Word of God. That is what is supposed to happen at a church. I felt as though he was talking directly to me. I too could lead, build, and teach, and I very much enjoyed doing all three. At that moment, I tapped Victoria on the shoulder and I said, "That's it! I am through fighting it. I am going to be a preacher."

The next couple of days spent waiting on the scheduled appointment with our pastor seemed to drag on forever. I have improved in the patience field by leaps and bounds, but when I get an idea in my head, waiting is not an option and I want to go full force right now. Finally, the day arrived and we met with the pastor. I explained that I felt the call to ministry and was ready to do whatever I had to do to start. At this time, I was pretty much thinking this was the only way to get started. As I stated before, my knowledge was limited due to being raised in the religious box.

The pastor informed me that I had just missed the deadline to enter the "process," but that I could unofficially be the associate pastor of the local church. This basically entailed filling in when the pastor was sick or otherwise absent. It was also said that I needed to build a résumé within the church, as this would help with the process. Now, I had been involved with the church for many years, but now it took on a whole new meaning. I started attending Bible study there, attending all board meetings, Bible school, and I also started a men's breakfast program and a youth camp, both of which were very successful. One thing I laugh about is that two other pastors were involved in this deal. Both stated that now that I had accepted the call, the devil would really be attacking me and trying to throw me off. They warned me not to be discouraged because I wouldn't be in the pulpit for at least a year. Well, they were definitely right on the first one, but that was old news for me. I had felt constantly under attack for years. They were very wrong on the second.

Our pastor became very ill a month or so down the road and was absent for a long time. Guess what? They said I wouldn't preach for a year, but God said no, and I was in the pulpit for a couple months. Then the pastor returned. A couple of Sundays went by, and I told Victoria that sitting in the pew was not working for me anymore. I had tasted preaching, and now I wanted more. Well, then the pastor was sick again, and there I was for another couple of months, preaching not one, but two churches. My father told me, "Son, you are going to have to calm down; you are going to kill that poor pastor." I thought this was funny, but God was here. He knew I had accepted His call and had a love for it, and He was not going to be told by any man that His chosen servant would not carry out His will. After this, I was called by the administration to fill in at other churches as well. So, the year I was told to plan on not being in the pulpit, I pretty much spent in the pulpit.

I cannot and don't take credit for the sermons that I delivered in that time, and still don't today. God was leading me, and He gave me the words and the opportunity to present them. He let me see things that could be used to teach others. Many of my past trials and works were subject matter in the sermons. I developed a following. Many people were surprised and eager to hear. Perhaps none was more surprised than me.

Further attacks soon came. Victoria and I were ready to be married, but I wouldn't pull the trigger because I was worried about finances. I wanted to be able to get her a nice ring, a nice wedding, and a stable home. I did not feel ready as a man to be able to provide those things. I was doing well just to support what we had. She didn't care, but I did; it was all part of that feeling inadequate thing again. Then we lost the house we were in. We had a handshake deal with an ex-family member and had done $10,000 worth of work on the place, and then he decided he needed to move back in. So once again, back to Mom and Dad's place. This was a blow.

Then to top it off, three weeks after deciding to go into the ministry, my business tanked for no reason. Jobs dropped off, the hands were dragging their feet, payroll was out of hand, and payments were slow. We had to shut down, close the office and go back to a one-man operation. Again, it all fell apart at once, but I kept my head up yet again because I knew God was in control and He was going to do great things with us. A lot of little things were happening around us reassuring me He was there. I had by now officially entered the process of becoming a pastor in the Methodist system. We were on the way up.

That family court mess was still lurking in the background, though.

# 5.  Eighteen Days in the Clink

**V**ictoria and I were working hard trying to calculate our next move. We were trying to figure out a place to stay on our own, how to make money, how to progress spiritually with this new path. I was working the few contracts I had left, alone, and she was traveling with her mother working. I had also become well aware that I needed to slow down and put in more time with God and the Bible if I was going into ministry. I had people texting me wanting answers, wanting to know when and where I was preaching next— people who were inspired and wanted to talk to me. I was also still preaching at church and had a ton of paperwork and stuff to do for the process I had entered. Not to mention I still had my duties as fire chief, president of the community center, a father fighting for his kids, and a man trying to get back on his feet. My family supported me all the way. Honestly, I expected some kickback when I said I was going to preach, but there was none.

I had a pending court date and a feeling that something bad was going to happen. I did not know exactly what, but I had a really uneasy feeling about it. Victoria had tried not to go out of town to work with her mother, but I talked her into it. I didn't let on that something bad was coming. At that time, I wondered how I knew that; now I know it was God talking to me. With all of this going on and Victoria out of town, I finally made time to be alone and pray about several things. I got off of a job early, went to the store and bought myself a six-pack...of boneless chicken thighs and a gallon jug of sweet tea, and off to the woods I went. I had a campsite with a swing grill and a fire pit. I lit a fire and set my chair next to it. I placed that chicken on the grill and began to drink my tea right out of the jug. I took a deep breath and started talking to God out loud. I had a long list of things that I needed, and I let Him have it.

- First and foremost, I thanked Him for the many blessings I had received and for the honor of being able to preach His Word and do His works. I also thanked Him for choosing me. I told Him I did not know why He had, but that I gladly accepted and would do what He asked.

- I needed clarity on a few people in my life. I was beginning to think they were wolves in sheep's clothing.

- I needed to know if Victoria was really the one this time or if she was another shyster coming into my life to cause me more chaos and heartache.

- I needed my family to be closer together and be tighter with one another like it used to be.

- I needed time to study the Bible and pray about this calling. I was too tied up with other things to truly give it the time it deserved.

- I needed to be closer to God and to be able to see Him at work so I could tell others.

- I needed guidance in this calling that would lead me to the right place where He wanted me.

- I prayed for my children and the whole court circus and the people in it.
- I prayed for my health to improve.

I talked to Him in this manner for at least an hour. I spent the rest of the night out there just thinking and reflecting. It was a very peaceful time and I felt the presence of God around me. I knew He was hearing me. Now, I'm going to tell you, that prayer up there, He answered in a huge way. I don't mean to make light of the situation, but this is one time I saw prayer work, and I learned to be more specific when speaking to the Lord.

This all occurred on a Friday. I don't remember what I did Saturday. Sunday I preached, and Monday afternoon at about two thirty, I was standing in a courtroom. Much to my surprise, one of my so-called friends showed up to court. This was a surprise, because I had told no one about having court. Remember earlier, when I said the opposing lawyer was friends with my friend? Court proceeded as usual: she tore me apart, except this time I had no lawyer because I had run out of money. They had finally bled me dry. The judge once again paused the proceedings because he had somewhere else to be, as usual. A document he asked me to bring at the last appearance was thrown out as hearsay, as usual.

He came back a short time later and said that I was to spend 180 days in the county jail because of the child support situation. *What? Me?* A servant of God, fire chief, former law enforcement, paramedic, good, hard-working family man in *jail?* I was in shock. I could not believe it. Of course, the shady lawyer who was fighting a complaint I had filed got her revenge, and the ex was smiling and happy. I said, "Well, what have you accomplished? Do you think I am going to find a pile of money over there in the jail to pay your ransom for my kids? You just took away any means I had of making money!" They didn't care, and neither did the corrupt judge who had taken my kids from me over false accusations, without trial, and with three separate investigating agencies clearing me of any wrong-doing. This judge had condemned me without hearing my side, and ultimately jailed me on a document that should have been thrown out as hearsay! I should have caught that; I am a smart man, but I was overcome with shock and anger and missed it. Of course, this was God answering my prayers, but I just did not know it at the time.

Now, I am not claiming to be an apostle by any means. But do you see the similarities? They were jailed, beaten, and run out of town on a regular basis for doing good works and exposing the lies and sins of the head priests. They healed the sick, raised the dead, cast out demons, preached the Word, and for what? The people threw them in jail. Any good person seeking God, a strong Christian or any other servant of God, will be attacked by evil. There will be obstacles and tests thrown your way in an attempt to keep you from or to turn you away from God. You must stay the course, remain in faith, and ask Him to help you endure the trial. It is much easier to endure when you bring Him along. You must remember that the Bible says He has already defeated Satan and He has conquered the world.

I hope by now you see that the attack on me is getting worse as this book progresses, but my attitude about it is better at this point because my faith and inclusion of God has progressed as well. You see, the closer I get to God, the more and stronger the attacks came. Do not be discouraged: this story is about to take a one-eighty. Buckle up and prepare to be amazed.

I had emptied my pockets onto my truck seat before I went in the courtroom. I had also left a folder with some important documents lying on the front seat. I had anticipated that if this did happen, all I would have is my truck key, which could be released from my property in jail, and the needed documents to work the bail situation out were in the truck. I had told no one of any of this: not my fiancée, not my parents. Wolf number two showed up to court as well. With that being said, I still had questions and trust, so my keys were given to them. I said where my dad was, and to call and let Victoria know what happened, and to get my truck home, and where the file folder was located. They agreed.

I was placed in handcuffs and taken from the courtroom to the jail—where I had been many times, just on the opposite side of the cuffs. Immediately, several people recognized me; you could see the surprised look on their faces. I was taken back to sick bay. This is an individual cell versus a cell with a group. I was extremely glad this happened. This was done, of course, because I used to work in law enforcement. Unfortunately for society, there is such a thing as repeat offenders, so I could not be put in population, which I was very thankful for.

There I was in what felt like a cardboard box. A very small room. The shock had not worn off yet, but still, I had expected to be released soon. We had planned for this possibility years ago when the drama started because we all knew she wouldn't stop until this happened. It was just her nature. Hours passed and nothing happened. Finally, Victoria was there. I was called up to talk on the phone and it was her. She was upset, as she should have been. She relayed to me that the bail situation would not work because of the way the lawyer had worded the paperwork. This was clue number three, as nobody else knew of the plan. It was also relayed to me that the folder was not in the truck, and that hours had passed and my father had not been notified. Clues four and five. See, God knows I'm a slow learner so He shows me multiple times. However, He wasn't through showing me that situation.

Now I became worried. I knew there was no money to fight this. I knew this was what she had been wanting for years, and here I was, sitting in a jail cell. I could see myself spending the next six months in jail, and that was not a good feeling. I am pretty good and stable, but let me tell you, when you are in a room you can't leave and there is no TV, telephone, book, pen, paper, not even a bathroom door, your world starts crashing pretty quick, and mine did. My anxiety took over and I began to worry. I tried to keep calm, but it wasn't working really well.

I sort of stepped back and went into survival mode. I took an assessment of what I had, which was time and space—which I did pray for, remember? I had a pencil and a piece of paper brought to me that I was not expecting. The first thing I drew was a cross. Next, I tried to make a calendar so I could keep track of time. I was trying not to go nuts by concentrating on getting set up and occupied. It did not dawn on me for quite some time that I should pray. Later that evening, my anxiety was kicking my butt. I realized that this was real, and I was stuck there. Finally it dawned on me again that I was not alone, so I began to pray. I prayed for calmness and to stop my anxiety. I prayed the same for Victoria, and I asked to find a way out of this place. Eventually, I fell asleep.

Around four thirty in the morning, they came and woke me up. I thought, *Good, something is happening*. They told me, "Well, it doesn't look like you are going to get out soon, so we need to get you booked in." There was some good news. So, I got the mug shot and the blue coveralls and the crappy socks and underwear and away I went, back to my hole. Breakfast came at five a.m. I don't remember what it was, but I'm guessing I ate it.

Again, I found myself trapped in this small room with nothing to do but worry about what was going on. What would this mean for my newly discovered calling and my involvement in the church? What would this mean for all of the positions I held in the community? What would people think of me now? I began to think that yet again, I had been stripped down to nothing. I soon realized that I had only one way to occupy my time, and that was to lean on God to help me out. Remember how earlier I had prayed for time to think about my calling and walk closer with God? This was that time I had asked for, although it would take me a few days to fully realize it.

I was given a piece of paper with a list of items that I could order during my stay. This consisted of things like a deck of cards, pens, paper, envelopes, deodorant, soap, telephone time, et cetera. This was on a Tuesday, and the order had to be placed by noon that day, but I did not have any money to make the order. I remember thinking that if I could just get some paper and something to write with, I could have something to do to occupy my time. Noon was drawing near, and I had already made up my mind that it would be a week more before I could have these things. I would have to wait until someone came to visit before I could ask them to put money into my account there. I was dreading and worrying about having to spend a week in solitude with nothing to occupy my mind. I was allowing that worry and stress to enter my mind and defeat me.

I did not see this at the time, but God was there. He heard the cries of my heart, He knew what I needed, and even though I did not turn to Him as I should have, He blessed me anyway. With just a few minutes to spare, I was informed that there had been some funds placed into my account and if I was to hurry, I could place an order.

I quickly ordered a legal pad, sketch paper, pens, colored pencils, deck of cards, deodorant, and shampoo. There were things on there such as candy bars and chips and such, but I was in survival mode. I ordered useful things, not snacks that would quickly come and go. I felt a sense of relief, knowing that if I could just hold out a couple more days, then I would be set.

Again, the prayer I prayed before asked to become closer to God and see Him work. At this moment in time, it didn't dawn on me, but He was answering my prayer yet again. He heard me, He came through at the last minute; He was there and worked it out. Later, I would see not only this, but many of His other works in my life both past and present. In most of my daily situations, I find that I pray for things—and sometimes I don't officially pray for them, just think or worry about them—He always provides, and usually waits until the final hour to do so. I think this is done to test my faith and teach me patience. When He solves a problem for me that I didn't actually take to Him, only thought or worried about, I realize at the moment of relief that I should have taken it to Him. This is a teachable moment in which He is trying to make me understand to take all my worries and anxieties to Him.

> *1 Peter 5:6-7 (NLT) So humble yourselves under the mighty power of God, and at the right time he will lift you up in honor. Give all your worries and cares to God, for he cares about you.*

This is a hard thing for many of us to do. We get into the mindset of "God doesn't have time for that" or "God has more important things to worry about." This could not be further from the truth. All of us are God's children, and He wants to take care of us and prosper us. Just like any father, He wants you to come to Him, seek Him, and love Him, which also means depending on Him. Those of you who are parents can relate. I sometimes hear parents saying, "Those kids depend on me for everything, always borrowing money, asking me to solve their problems," et cetera. Deep down, though, even as some parents complain about it, there is a great feeling of love and honor when your children come to you for help. You are the one who can show your love by helping them. It is a great feeling to know you are their rock, their shelter, the one they can depend on.

So why would your Heavenly Father feel any different? The Bible tells us throughout to come to Him, and He loves us, so why not let Him? Many will miss the opportunity to see God at work. The above situation could have easily been explained away by circumstance, coincidence, or just plain luck. Do not let the evil one fool you and lead you astray from the works of God. You must understand that when your needs are met in "the final hour" such as this, that it was God in action. The people who put money in my account didn't know my needs, they did not know of my anxiety, they did not know of my plan to buy these things, nor did they know about the dead-line. However, God knew all of these things and made it happen. *Luck, coincidence, circumstance*—those are all words we use to define situations or happenings, but they are just words. *God* is real, more than just a word, and He is at work in your life every second of every day. Many label His works as luck or coincidence. It is time to open your eyes and realize what God is doing in your life.

Having the order placed did ease my mind a bit, but I still had several periods of anxiety and fear. One evening when I was wound up and bored out of my mind, it finally dawned on me to pray about it. I asked for peace and for relief from the worries of my mind, and in just a few minutes, it began to ease. I began to concentrate on other things. When I found myself getting wound up, I would pace around the room. I began to do push-ups against the wall several times a day.

During all of this, I would get to talk to family for thirty minutes at a time on Sunday and Wednesday mornings via a video phone in a conference room. I began to look forward to these times. Several times I was asked if I wanted to go to the TV room or to step outside into the fenced-in area for some fresh air. I went to the TV room once and to the outside area a couple times. I didn't like doing either of these things, mainly because I did not want to be seen by anyone. Once it dawned on me to pray about it, I began to pray a lot to relieve my worries. Soon after, they eased. I began to understand more and more about the power of prayer and that God was listening.

A couple of days later, the supplies I ordered arrived in the morning. I was happy and thought that I was set now. I could write down my thoughts, do some drawing, and maybe play some solitaire. Well, that lasted about two hours, I guess. I found that my mind was so wound up, I could write nothing. I wrote a poem, which I do not do. It just flowed out; it was about the current situation I was in. That did not take but just a few minutes, or so it seemed. So, then it was back to the normal routine of pacing around, doing push-ups, sitting and trying to draw, and then back up again. I found myself praying a lot now for peace and to get this situation resolved. The calmness seemed to last for a while, and then I found myself praying again.

Meanwhile, outside those walls, my family was coming together. They had contacted an attorney and began the steps to undo this mess. They were planning and figuring out how to get enough money rounded up to pay the lawyer and the ransom to get me out of jail. The family was coming together well, just as I had prayed for before this started. They seemed to be working around the clock. I realized even more that I was loved and missed, even though I was in this mess. They had secured the lawyer and the money, and then the real fight began.

The opposing attorney started playing hard to find. She would agree to a meeting and then not be there. They would finally get her tracked down, and then she would wait for days to review the paperwork and then send it back for some trivial thing like a word or punctuation. She was doing anything she could to delay the process and keep it as difficult as possible. I was told several times that I should be out that day, or tomorrow, or next week. It kept changing; she was playing all the lawyer games she could just to cause problems. She was trying her best to keep me in until after Christmas, but her plan was foiled finally.

In the end, my fiancée suggested to my father that he should call my ex and let her know that the money was at her lawyer's office, that it had been for nearly two weeks now, and that her lawyer was delaying the process. As it turns out, she did not even know the money was available; the lawyer had not told her. It was just the lawyer playing evil games for spite. Just as we knew all along, my ex jumped at the money. In the final hour on a Friday afternoon, just before they all shut down for the holidays, I was finally released from jail.

Although the lawyer was the one delaying the process, making my stay in solitude longer, it was all part of God's plan. He was doing a work in me as well as in others in my life. He was using a bad event in our lives to work for His and our good. I was learning that prayer really worked and that He was listening. One day I was pacing in my cell. There was a door on each end of the cell and a shower stall on the side. I was pacing back and forth, praying for God to take me out of there and get this resolved. At one time, I was leaning against one of the doors with my hands on the frame above my head and I was saying, "I know You can blow these doors open whenever You get ready." I then thought, *As a matter of fact, I'm going to step into the shower stall so that I am not between the doors when You blow them open.* Some will say I am making this up, but it is true. Just as I stepped into that stall, the locks on both doors popped and opened. An officer was standing in each door, and there I was looking like a fool standing in the shower stall.

One officer had two letters that my family had written me, and the other had a stack of books that my family had sent me. I was in awe but still not free. This was a huge relief to me for a couple of reasons. One, it was nice to read the letters and see what they were saying. Two, I now had books to occupy my time. The books were a Bible, a daily devotional book, and the *Lonesome Dove* novel.

Now my time had changed. I had the daily devotional, which made it much easier to keep track of days and time. I had the Bible for study and the novel for recreation. I now set my schedule for the day. I would get up around 5:00 a.m. when breakfast came. I would eat and read the devotional for the day. I would then sit and think about that for a bit. After that, I considered my new job to be in ministry, so I started to read the Bible from page one. I would read the Bible all day, taking a short break around noon when they brought lunch. I would use the legal pad I had to make notes and write down Scripture. Dinner would come around 5:00 p.m., or so I was told. I had no way of keeping time other than when they brought meals. I could not tell between day and night, as there was a light on twenty-four-seven and no way to see outside. After dinner, I would usually set the Bible down and begin reading the novel until I fell asleep. Sometimes I would continue to read the Bible for a bit.

This was my day every day. In between, I would take breaks to pace around or do my makeshift push-ups off the wall. I spent almost all of my time in there reading. I wrote down several Scriptures, some to make sermons out of, others that just seemed to fit or interest me at the time. Having these books made the days go by easier, but I was still ready to get out of there.

The area I was in was referred to as sick bay. These are cells where someone who was ill could be separated from everyone else. They were also used as a disciplinary measure. If someone acted up, they were placed in there alone, I guess as a form of punishment. I heard them being moved in and out and could hear discussions, which was what led me to this assumption. Although I had once worked there, I was not familiar with the jail operations; I was not in that division. I would hear them cussing and screaming at the officers and each other. This, as you may imagine, never worked out well for the inmate. They just got into more trouble by doing that. When I would hear this I would start praying for them, mainly for God to work in them and give them an understanding that yelling was not going to solve the problem. I would pray for peace in them, safety for all, or anything else I may have been able to deduce at the time about them or their situation. Before long, all of the yelling and cussing came to an end in the hallway. They were all still there, but all the yelling, cussing, arguing, and such had ended. God was again showing me that prayer worked.

In my prayer before this happened, I had asked for time to study the Bible and think about my calling more. Well, He gave me about fourteen straight days to do that, basically uninterrupted. I asked Him to let me get closer to Him and see Him at work. Well, He brought me closer because He was all I had in there. He let me see Him work by seeing the power of prayer, opening those doors, and reading His Word. Many other things were happening outside, which I would learn of and experience later. I asked for my family to draw closer together, which they did. I asked for Him to reveal the wolves to me, which He plainly did. I asked to see if Victoria was the real one, and she most definitely was; He made that clear as well.

I had asked to restore my health, and He did. I lost weight while I was in there. Also, before I went in, I was having chest pains and shortness of breath along with swelling in my lower extremities. This was being treated as mild congestive heart failure. By the time I was released, the swelling had gone away, and my breathing had improved. Now, I am not taking the credit away from God, but that probably had a lot to do with my new diet and the fact that I was doing the push-ups and a lot of walking back and forth. He also placed me in an environment where I had time to walk and do the push-ups and my diet was controlled, so He gets credit for that too. The final part about leading me to where I was supposed to be in my calling was about the only thing left out in the open at that point, but He gave me some insight on that as well.

One night while I was pacing around and just making random comments and praying, He placed an idea into my head. I was going to head up a ministry for divorced fathers and/or those whose children had been taken from them. He said I was going to have a big building with counselors and a legal staff, including attorneys who would be at my disposal. Fathers like myself who had been stripped of all of their finances, lost their children, and been destroyed by the family court system would come to me. We would evaluate their circumstances and then sit them in a room in a nice big chair, and my staff would go to work to right the wrong free of charge. I'm talking about bringing in the big guys who would ram right through the nonsense, right the terrible wrongs committed, and restore the father to his children. Meanwhile, there would be a church in place there as well to bring people to Jesus during the process. Other fathers who came in, those who might actually have issues in their past that could have legitimately led to the situation they were in, could be helped too. We would have counselors for them, groups with other fathers whom they could speak with and learn from. There was to be a qualified meeting place and system that would be approved by the courts. This would be a place where real visitation could take place in a father-friendly environment, where you were not treated like a convict for being a male.

All of this sounded really nice to me, as there was a real need for a ministry like this. I only had one question, and that was how in the world I would pay for it. Immediately, it came back to me to start preaching and posting videos to the internet. I was also to write a book about my calling to the ministry. (The book you are reading now!) My fiancée and I were directed to write a book together about the experience of the two of us meeting, how we dealt with the family courts, and how we came to ministry. He said the video would go viral, the books would sell, and there would be the money. I am working on making that happen.

When I got out, I immediately established the Fathers in Faith page on both YouTube and Facebook. There are a couple of videos there, but that will come later.

# 6. What Now?

I think it was around 4:30 p.m. when an officer opened the door to my cell and said, "What are we supposed to be doing?" By this time, I had been hearing that I was "going to get out today" for three days.

I said, "I'm not sure."

She said, "All they told me was to come get you."

Hoping for the best, I said, "I'm going home then."

I gathered my belongings and we made our way to the front desk. I changed back into my clothes, got my things, and took my tail through that door for the last time. Victoria and her mother were waiting to take me home. They told me all about how the opposing lawyer had been trying to make a problem and how it almost didn't happen. Victoria told me she was sitting in the church and God told her that today was the day. It was late in the day, just before everyone was leaving the office for the holidays, and He made it happen.

We made the rounds and visited with everyone for what would prove to be several very emotional reunions. My nieces and nephews were scared to death of me being gone. My mother was a wreck, and so was Victoria. My ninety-one-year-old grandmother just held my hand and cried for what seemed like an eternity. This experience lit a new fire in me. I was closer than I ever had been with God, I had a clear view of the enemy and what he was capable of, and I knew who he worked through. I was ready to do battle.

My business was essentially closed now. You can't just be absent for eighteen days and expect to retain customers. My ego was shot; although I felt close with God, my earthly life was pretty much over as far as I thought. I was not sure at all what to do next. The only thing I knew was that I was going to preach the Word of God. My standing in the church remained the same, and very soon I found myself back in the pulpit as if nothing had happened. I established the Facebook page and placed a few sermons on there. I also officially began the process of becoming a local pastor with the United Methodist Church.

In the meantime, Victoria and I were back at my parents' house for a while, then with my brother, and eventually we moved into her family's home. We got by with me doing small jobs here and there and working for her mother's business, traveling around doing shows and making things for her. I was preaching and working with the church on various things, going to meetings, reading more books and studying. At one of the shows we went to in Mobile, Alabama, I actually got to get up on the stage and give a short message to about 200 people. For the rest of the day, people kept coming by the booth saying how meaningful it was to them, which made me feel good. I knew God was still using me for His purpose.

However, we were just living; I didn't feel as though I was making any progress. I kept thinking, *I need to be doing something*, but I couldn't really complain. I felt as though I wasn't working, but I really was, just not making any financial progress for my family. We had housing, we were well fed, and we were getting by—but that is all. I felt much like the disciples when Jesus sent them out.

*Matthew 10:10 (NLT) Don't carry a traveler's bag with a change of clothes and sandals or even a walking stick. Don't hesitate to accept hospitality, because those who work deserve to be fed.*

I could clearly see that although I was officially unemployed, I was still working for what was being given to me, and I was doing God's work in the ministry. This verse gave me some comfort, but I felt I needed to be doing more.

I was progressing in the process with the church. I was being told all kinds of things about getting to go preach, meeting people, and going to meetings. I began to feel as if something big was about to happen, yet I still didn't feel 100 percent confident that I was moving in the right direction. It all sounded good, but I found too many holes in the conversation. One person would say one thing and make one promise, while someone else would contradict it. Then I would read something that blew both sides out of the water. Then something completely random and out of place would happen. It was just wishy-washy to me and did not feel right. I felt as though it was an unorganized deal and that I could trust no one. I kept moving forward, though.

Our pastor, who was helping me along with this deal, met me one night and informed me that she was leaving to go to another church. Immediately I had it in my mind that I was going to be asked to finish out the rest of the year until they reassigned everyone. After all, I was traveling all over filling in for other churches. Our congregation seemed to be happy with it. There were several people asking when and where I would be preaching next or when I would be posting something. I was told that they were bringing in a man to fill the position, and I would be filling in for a couple weeks or so until he started. This was kind of a letdown but not the end of the world for me. It just confused me further and weakened my faith in this organization because there was too much conflicting information.

The new pastor-to-be moved into the parsonage. As in the past, several of us went and helped unload and set up for them. I had a chance to meet with him. I explained what my former role was in the church under the previous pastor and what I was willing to do. I made it very clear, in my mind anyway, that he was in charge now and would use me however he saw fit. He told me he wasn't here to change anything, that he planned for me to have a big role in the operation, and he would help train me, et cetera. Later on, he revealed to me that I would be preaching once per quarter and he would watch from the pew and give me advice. That sounded okay to me. This only happened one time, which was okay.

I took him around to make visits in the community one day, just to show him around town and where everyone lived and such. We made three stops and people were glad to see him, but then they started talking about me and what I was doing in the church. I could tell this was a problem, but neither of us said anything about it. The day was cut short; I took him back to his house and went on my way. I told Victoria then that there would most likely be trouble in paradise.

Moving forward, I was still receiving a ton of conflicting information. I had three different pastors and their supervisor all telling me different things. One said I would never preach; one said it would be any minute now; another said this or that. It was just chaos, and I began to worry even more that I was moving in the wrong direction. I was told that I would be starting an outreach ministry type of deal at our church. I met with the pastor of the church and one from another church and began training for the position. One pastor was telling me to move forward and that he was expecting to hear results, while the other was telling me to hold off and that he was going to put someone else in charge of the thing. I was being told no by the pastor at our church and being asked why I wasn't moving by the pastor training me, which left me in the middle looking like a fool. It isn't like these two didn't communicate; they met at least once a week, it seemed. I didn't want to rock the boat. There was trouble brewing, I had seen it all too much in the past, and this time I was the one caught in the middle.

I was feeling very strongly that God was showing me all of this trying to expose the complications of man-made doctrine, which I really didn't realize existed until now. There was deception and back-stabbing, lies being told, confusion, all the makings of trouble—the last thing you would expect in what was supposed to be something so simple. I began to feel very strongly that God was leading me to walk away and start our own ministry.

Then I found a post on Facebook where a local rest home was searching for someone to come in and do a service on Sunday morn-ing. I saw this as a golden opportunity for someone like me to get my feet wet, so to speak, as an aspiring pastor while helping others. I could have taken this task on myself, as I had already checked with the powers governing the doctrine of the church and the process, and they had said it was fine as long as I didn't identify myself as representing them. (Huh? I represented them on several Sundays in four different churches already!)

I was formerly in public safety where chain of command is essential. With that in mind, I checked with the new pastor of our church to see if it would be okay. He said no, that we were not ready for that. He said he would have to investigate their needs and check it all out, et cetera, et cetera. I found this strange. I thought the

Bible said we were all baptized into the body of Christ, which is the church. One church. I didn't think it, I knew it. I had read it myself.

> *Ephesians 4:4-6 (NLT) For there is one body and one spirit, just as you have been called to one glorious hope for the future. There is one Lord, one faith, one baptism, one God and Father of all, who is over all, in all, and living through all.*

> *Colossians 1:18 (NLT) Christ is also the head of the church, which is his body. He is the beginning, supreme over all who rise from the dead. So he is first in everything.*

> *Acts 11:26 (NLT) When he found him, he brought him back to Antioch. Both of them stayed there with the church for a full year, teaching large crowds of people. (It was at Antioch that the believers were first called Christians.)*

I had been baptized and had become a Christian. This made me part of the *church*, or body of Christ, and I wanted to spread the gospel. We are charged with this duty:

> *Matthew 28:18-20 (NLT) Jesus came and told his disciples, "I have been given all authority in heaven and on Earth. Therefore, go and make disciples of all the nations, baptizing them in the name of the Father, and the Son, and the Holy Spirit. Teach these new disciples to obey all the command I have given you. And be sure of this: I am with you always, even to the end of the age."*

This right here is where I really started to throw the brakes on. The Bible said one thing and man was saying another. If I am ever forced to choose whose rules I am going to follow, I will always choose what is written in the Bible: the words written there inspired by God. As a matter of fact, the quotations in Matthew 28 are the words of Jesus Himself. Who did they think they were to go against the word of Jesus Himself? Let me sum this up for you. I was a believer. I was baptized, which brought me into the body of Christ, being the Church, which makes me a Christian, and Jesus said, "Go forth and make disciples of all nations." That is what God says in the Scriptures; but the heads of what they call a "church" said no, you can't say you are representing the church, you cannot go and spread the gospel. We are not ready for that. Let me translate this again to what they said: We are the self-righteous heads of an organization that pushes man-made doctrine using the name of Jesus, and you aren't qualified to play in our house. Now that is what I heard when I cut through all of the nonsense about legalities and qualifications. Jesus had something to say about this too:

> **Matthew 7:21-23 (NLT) Not everyone who calls out to me "Lord! Lord!" will enter the Kingdom of Heaven. Only those who actually do the will of my Father in Heaven will enter. On judgement day, many will say to me "Lord! Lord! We prophesied in your name and cast out demons in your name and performed many miracles in your name." But I will reply, I never knew you. Get away from me, you who break God's laws.**

I really began to get worried at this point. I already had the go-ahead from the person I technically answered to in the organization, so I knew if I proceeded in doing this I would not be jeopardizing the possibility of completing the process. That was important to me in case that completion was what God wanted. So I started doing the service at the rest home about one month later.

At this point, I really felt that I was on the wrong road following the local church. It was not the place I thought it was. God was beginning to teach me that I had been misled in many ways in the past forty years there. He was also showing me the true colors of many more people, the wolves in sheep's clothing again. The new pastor began to slowly put up obstacles to slow down my work within the church. I was becoming greatly disappointed and quickly losing confidence in the church.

One day when I was supposed to go to a training meeting, I received a call from the district superintendent who oversaw all of the pastors and such other things. She asked me if I could come in early and meet with her. Because of what I was being told all this time, I thought they were about to assign me to a church somewhere. I knew there were a couple openings that were formerly filled with those in the process. The closer I got, the more I thought about it and questioned what I should do. I prayed to God and asked that He would make it clear what I should do if this was not the path He had chosen for me.

Now, you must understand that up to this point, all those involved were calling and encouraging me. We were meeting for dinner, I was filling in at places, all was moving forward. When I arrived for the meeting, she was holding a manila envelope. She slid it across the table to me and said that she was about to assign me a church, but the bishop had denied it. She said that my credit score was an embarrassment to me, God, and the church. She said as long as that was the case, I could not be given a church to pastor.

I was immediately infuriated; this was crazy to me. Where in the Bible had Jesus run credit reports before calling people to the ministry? Furthermore, I was again being punished without the chance to speak and explain my side of the deal. The ex had played a big part in causing my credit to plummet, so once again, she was holding me back and attempting to destroy me. I did state that the credit report had old information that had been settled with a Chapter 13 bankruptcy. This had been completed, all were paid back, and I had a credit attorney working to clear the old information. They were not interested in the details, just the number. I started to walk out there and then. I had asked God to show me, and He had. I still did not want to make any hasty decisions, though. I decided that I would wait to make a decision about withdrawing from the process for thirty days. There would be plenty of time for prayer and more direction to follow. Again, I surprised myself, as I was learning patience and letting God be in control, all of which was new for me.

This would not be the only sign He would show me that day. One of the steps I had to take in the process was getting the local pastor-parish relations committee of my church to endorse me as a candidate. I had looked at my booklet and read the discipline (man-made rule book of the organization), and all it said was exactly what I just said: that I needed to schedule a meeting to receive their endorsement. Now, again, all I had to do was make a phone call and set this up, but being respectful of the chain of command, I had contacted this new pastor to let him in on the plan before I called anyone. I asked him what I needed to do, and all he said to me was this: "I could tell you, John, but I am not. You need to learn to start using the discipline and look these things up yourself." Again, I had already done that. I was just trying to play nice and bow to the authority he thought he had over me. Once again, my attempts to play nice were met with rudeness and conflict. This conversation had taken place a week or so before the day I met with the district superintendent. It just so happened that God knew what was coming. He already knew I was going to be praying to be shown His will, so He aligned both events to happen on the same day.

I drove straight in from the first meeting of the day to the church where the second meeting was to take place. On one hand, I was infuriated. I did not understand how these people thought this was okay, but I knew God was at work. I sat down at the table, as I had arrived about an hour early, and I began to search the Scriptures. I found nothing at all about credit score, financial standing, education, or pretty much anything else that stopped Jesus from calling people to ministry. If He wanted you, He got you. As a matter of fact, I read a lot about just the opposite. Social standing, finances, or men of earthly position meant nothing when Jesus was calling.

People began to arrive for the meeting. I smiled, pretending all was well. The meeting was progressing well; the chair of the committee walked in with the approval letter in hand, as we all knew what the vote would be. I had been working in that church for forty years and had been in the pulpit regularly for the past several months. As I expected, the pastor walked in with the Book of Discipline. He must have had at least twenty Post-it tabs hanging out of the side of it. As soon as they asked for the vote he stopped them, saying the process they were taking was all wrong. He said I was supposed to answer several questions, write a paper, and jump through all of these hoops.

I pointed out the fact that I had asked him these questions and he had refused to answer. I was also confused, as I had looked in the discipline as well and did not see any of this. An argument of facts ensued, and at the end of that it was determined that he had a version of the discipline that was several years old and no longer valid. His attempt to throw a stumbling block had failed, and the motion passed unanimously. Once that was done, I took the letter of endorsement and placed it in my folder. I thanked the committee for their vote of confidence. I then began to explain the events earlier in the day and that it appeared as though I would not be put forward in the process.

Of course, the pastor broke out his book again and began explaining how I was not qualified and what the discipline said. It probably was not the most Christian conversation, but I guess it was necessary. I pointed out that the discipline was a man-made rule book and did not outrank what God was saying. He retorted saying the book was written by men ordained by God. I retorted saying men ordained by God according to the process written by their man-made book. I ended it by sliding my Bible to the center of the table and saying, "That book was actually written by God, so find it in there." At that point the conversation ended.

The following month was pretty quiet in the church as far as my involvement. The daily conversations that were taking place came to an abrupt halt. The filling in that was scheduled was canceled. Many things were happening in my life that were constantly guiding me to start a church. People were calling asking where I would be, et cetera. I pretty much had my mind made up, but I was going to hold out the thirty days before I made the decision.

On the last day, the day before my next meeting, an offer was made to me by the pastor who had come down from the administration. I was to assemble a congregation and meet in a local church that was dwindling away. There were two stipulations: I couldn't take anyone from either church, and I could not schedule things at times that would interfere with either existing congregation. I thought that this might be God talking again, so I put my plans to withdraw on hold again and began to move forward organizing this new venture.

A few weeks went by. I had the times and everything set so I took the information to the pastor. He then informed me that this new venture had been placed on hold as there was now another project in the works. Again, more confusion, and the left hand not knowing what the right hand was doing. God had called me to the ministry, and once again I was being held back by man from answering my calling. Again, I was led to believe that I was to go my own way, to follow my call in another direction, but I still held on.

A few weeks later, here came another offer from them. They offered me a part-time position with a new ministry they were starting. I was to work with another pastor and help with a ministry for those struggling with addiction. I was offered a small monthly salary and a place to live. I turned down the place to live, which I will talk about in a bit, but I accepted the position. It was not at all what I wanted to do, but at this point I was not going to turn down anything God put before me until I knew for sure. I did make sure, however, that if I withdrew from the process, it would not affect this offer. They assured me that one had nothing to do with the other.

By now I was married to Victoria and we had a child on the way. I made the decision to withdraw from the process, but I carried on with the new position. I was making my mind up to start a church, but I was stalling. Victoria's mother came to us and said that Victoria's brother was to be married and they wanted me to perform the service at their home. I did some research and discovered that for this to be legal, I had to be an ordained minister somewhere. I found a place online in Dallas that would do this. I researched them, filled out some papers, made a phone call, sent a check, and received a license, good for one year, that made it legal to perform their wedding and sign the certificate for them to file.

Long story short, it ended up moving to the church building. I knew that if I tried to do the service they would say no, so again in order not to stir the pot, I did it anyway, at my own risk. By this point, I really did not care what they said about it. I had clearly been shown that all of my experience with them was basically a joke, and I was going to go my own way. Even this new venture was wishy-washy in my eyes. I knew that many, many other pastors, ministers, online people, et cetera, had performed weddings in that building with no issue. I knew that if I brought it up, the rule book would be thrown at me regardless of what anyone said after the fact. This was already proven to me on the most miniscule of matters such as getting a letter, so why would this be any different? This would cause trouble with the family and the church. I said it would be better for one man to face any fight rather than have several families and people involved in the upcoming turmoil. So I carried on with the wedding as if nothing was wrong. This was to be their time.

The following Monday I was called in by the pastor and told that I had broken the rules, et cetera. I was told that my offer of employment was withdrawn—real heartbreaker there—that I would never again be in the pulpit at any Methodist church, and that I was not allowed to be involved in any ministerial work in the church. Oh well, big deal. I was so put out with their nonsense that I didn't want to be a part of the circus anymore anyway. God had finally pushed me, since I was so slow to act, into going my own way. My time with the local church was over, and a new venture was on the horizon.

# 7.  A New Direction

About this time, my grandmother passed away. Not the one I mentioned before, but my other one. This was a bad situation, but it worked out. I'll spare you all of the details of this, but I will take a time out to tell you a little about life outside of the ministry at that point.

Victoria and I were still struggling with what we were going to do. We were taken care of, but in my mind, this was no way for two grown adults to be living. We both knew we were going to be married. My pride was keeping me from it, although everyone was telling me it was okay. Like I said before, I did not have the financial ability to buy what I thought was a proper ring, and I did not have a place of our own, et cetera. Victoria had told me before that God had told her that we needed to start the ministry, get married, and then we would have a child (a child she wanted badly). So, we did it.

Now, all of this was transpiring while the events in the last chapter were playing out. I'm telling one story of the life inside the church and calling, and another story of the other side, happening simultaneously, about Victoria and me. We started the new church, Living Discipleship Ministries, in March. We were also married in March, and then the baby was on the way, just like God had told her. We were able to purchase my grandmother's home and land. This was the perfect scenario. We were finally being obedient to God's calling. I had stepped away from the stumbling blocks. He let us be married, gave us a child, and gave us a home and land. We were seeing God work and take care of us daily.

I again fired up my contracting business and the jobs rolled in. It was amazing. He brought us customers, income, and allowed me to purchase equipment that I never dreamed of having, in cash. His blessings were flowing in constantly. The drama of family court still lingered over our heads. However, I soon realized that once again, I was focusing on business and losing focus on the ministry. I was moving the ministry, but not giving it the full time that it deserved. Just like before, the business suddenly fell due to a set of unrealistic events. In a few weeks, I found myself selling contracts and equipment and back to financial ground zero. At this point, I caved to the fact that I just needed to focus on the ministry full time and let God have control of everything else. So far, as I expected and knew He would, He *is* taking care of it all.

A few months after one grandmother passed, the other grandmother, the one I spoke of before, also passed. This was a tough one. God was definitely there at the time of her passing. She was surrounded by family. The family wanted me involved in the funeral process, which would put me back in the pulpit for a bit at the local church. This didn't fly well with them, but I did not care at all. By now there were several rumors flying around about how I was supposedly destroying the church and all kinds of things. That new pastor couldn't stop taking verbal shots at me even during this time. I turned the other cheek, just as the Book instructs us to. I was not the only one who made this observation; several have seen and heard what I am speaking of.

The new church was growing and moving. We were averaging about twenty to twenty-five each Sunday, along with fifteen to twenty-two or so at the rest home, and most of the online sermons being viewed near or above one hundred times per week. We had grown to around 138 followers on our Facebook page. I was pretty excited about this, but there was much more in store.

While all of this good was happening with the family and the new church development, there was an army forming against me in the local church and the community. A group of about six people, whom I recognized as wolves earlier, were spreading all kinds of turmoil. I would hear something new almost daily. It was a terrible thing but sort of comical at the same time. I was watching the devil work yet be defeated all the time. I maintained the high road. I could have engaged several times, but I was above all of that now. I made sure that I didn't do anything in the new church that was competing with the other. I made sure that times did not conflict. I wouldn't do certain things because I didn't want it to appear as though I was trying to start trouble.

Even at that, there was still talk. Each day I was hearing something new. The pastor would take verbal shots at me in a public forum at every opportunity. This did not work to his advantage; it ended with him making a fool of himself. This is actually the first time I have spoken of any of these details other than to family and close new friends. I have seen that evil needs to be exposed. If it is just accepted and not exposed, it only grows. Most sheep are just that. They do not want conflict so they go with the flow. I get it. But I have also seen God at work and the battle is His; we need only be still and give it to Him. It works.

The family court and the situation with my children were not going well. Shortly after I got out of jail, I had lawyers telling me they were going to fix this thing. More money was paid, and a supervised visit finally happened once for thirty minutes. I jumped through all of their hoops, but the court appearance never came. I was assured that things were moving forward. One year later I again contacted them. The case had been transferred to another attorney in the office who basically started from zero. They wanted me to jump through all the same hoops again: another home study, another evaluation, so on and so forth. Then they sent me another invoice.

Honestly, at this point, I am flat out of money and can no longer fight. All I can do is put it into God's hands. I pray daily for this situation to resolve. I miss my children terribly. I know they are being told all kinds of bad things about me, and by this point, after four years, I am hoping they are not thinking I have abandoned them. I cannot afford to fight. All I do is pray over it. I know now that God is making something good out of this evil work that has formed against me. He has molded me and is going to allow me to help others with this situation that they may also face. I get it, I'm trying to be strong, but it is hard.

Before long, I realized that the ministry was strong, God was moving, but I felt as if things had stalled. We were not really growing much and not doing much service work. Victoria and I discussed this at length. We finally came to the conclusion that I was doing the church a disservice by limiting our programs and walking on eggshells trying not to offend the other church. I was trying to do everything possible to avoid conflict, yet it was coming anyway. It was at this point that I decided I was going to move forward. This ministry was a church, too. The congregation was looking for things to happen. They did not deserve to be left out because someone else might not like what we were doing. I don't think God was smiling on that either. We were doing God's work, progressing His word and works. Who was I to put a limit on that? So we changed gears and jumped forward. His works became stronger, and we began to grow again. Here is the motivation that led to that leap forward.

I did feel a bit out of my comfort zone. I knew what God had told me to do; the messages I was delivering for Him were good—so I was being told. I had never run a church before. I had been in a supervisory role several times, I knew how to lead, I knew how to manage people, but I had never run a church. Many people reassured me and encouraged me. A man from the community came to me one day and asked about the church and why I started it. I automatically went into defense mode, assuming that this was yet another community member who had been led astray. I began to give a simple outline of how the church came about, saying that I did not agree with what was happening in the other church and that I had decided to move on, as I felt God was calling me to do so. He said he would like to talk about the matter further at another time. We agreed to meet and talk.

This turned into a weekly Bible study between him and me and sometimes Victoria. We started going over the book of Acts. Acts covers the beginning of the first church. God sent me this man to guide and reassure me. As we began our study, I saw Scriptures in a whole new light: everything we were doing in the church was following Acts exactly. This gave me a newfound knowledge and confidence. The fact that I am letting God lead me and sticking with Acts is why I think the church took a huge leap forward in the next few months.

Now that we mention the book of Acts, I am reminded of a meeting I was called to during this time with the pastor of the local church. This was a meeting that was supposed to clear the air, I guess. It was the first time we had met since all of the nonsense transpired. I remember praying on the way to this meeting, asking that God would keep me from losing my temper, give me strength to resist any slanderous remarks made toward me, and to help me live up to the way He would want me to respond.

I walked into the meeting and sat down. I noticed a few minutes in that the man was actually trembling; he hated me so much that he was actually shaking at the sight of me. This lasted about an hour or so. You know how people will be talking down to you and trying to slice you to pieces, but they do it with a smile and without actually saying the negative words? Kind of like the Southern saying "bless your heart"? That is exactly what was happening here. I looked around the room, a local diner, and noticed that the opposing lawyer I mentioned earlier was there, as well as the judge and a couple of other people who had crossed paths with me in the past. I remember feeling like Daniel in the lion's den at that point.

The thing that stood out to me in this meeting was when he relayed a conversation he had with someone regarding the new ministry Victoria and I had started. He said, "John meets at a building in town and talks with a group of people and takes money from them." This was the result of a past discussion where we were at odds over whether or not a building was a church. I said the building wasn't the church, but the people were (which is in the Scripture). He did not want to acknowledge the fact that we were holding a church in "the building." He wanted to make it seem like I was robbing people because it couldn't have been a church, because my credit score was bad and I didn't have a degree in theology, et cetera, et cetera. In my mind I said, *Yep, that is exactly what we are doing. Just like Peter in Acts chapter two, just like the first church, just as God has made it. Thanks for noticing.* To grasp this concept, you need to read Acts chapter two, but here are a few exerts from it to make my point.

*Acts 2:14 (NLT) Then Peter stepped forward with the eleven other apostles and shouted to the crowd, "Listen carefully, all of you, fellow Jews and residents of Jerusalem! Make no mistake about this."*

He then began to speak of the gospel of Jesus Christ.

*Acts 2:41 (NLT) Those who believed what Peter said were baptized and added to the church that day—about 3,000 in all.*

*Acts 2:42 (NLT) All the believers devoted themselves to the apostles' teaching, and to fellowship, and to sharing in meals (including the Lord's Supper), and to prayer.*

*Acts 2:44-47 (NLT) And all the believers met together in one place and shared everything they had. They sold their property and possessions and shared the money with those in need. They worshiped together at the temple each day, met in homes for the Lord's Supper, and shared their meals with great joy and generosity—all the while praising God and enjoying the goodwill of all the people. And each day the Lord added to their fellowship those who were being saved.*

I was proud of the fact that he said that. What was intended to berate the church was actually reassuring me. Peter gave the first sermon after Jesus was taken up into Heaven. He felt the call, just as I did. He went down and met with a group of people at a building in town and talked to them about Jesus Christ—just as I did. Those who believed were added to the church, just as we were doing. The people devoted themselves to the teaching and shared meals—just as we do every Sunday morning. All of the believers sold their belongings and brought monies to the church—just as we do; and they gave it to those in need, again, just as we do. So yes, I meet with a group of people at a building in town, and I do talk to them about Jesus. We break bread and have fellowship, and if they have an abundance, they give it to the church or someone in need, just as we are instructed to do in the Bible. The one difference that I can observe is this: Peter probably did not hesitate and put off the calling to do this as long as I had.

When that meeting was over, I stepped out of that building onto the sidewalk, and in my mind I said, *Lord, You really tested me there, didn't You? The room was filled with adversaries, harsh words were spoken at me, and You strengthened me and gave me a new outlook on the church You have led me to start.* I thanked Him for this. In my mind, I heard Him say, *Do not be intimidated by these people. You do not need their approval or counsel, so stop seeking it. I am with you.* All I can say is *wow*.

We had a revival over two days and saw around seventy-five people in attendance. I was going to get equipment to start a podcast, but one of my jobs didn't go the way I planned. I had to use the monies elsewhere, so I had to delay the podcast. At the revival, not only was enough money given to purchase the podcast equipment, but a lot of other equipment as well. We were also able to bless a couple people who needed to be blessed. God was working again in a very visible way.

We are now able to produce higher-quality videos and distribute them around to those who need to hear the Word. Our ability to increase our online presence is expanding. All of our equipment is mobile; we can set up anywhere. We have plans to do events this year and go out into the community to reach people.

We see God moving all the time here. One of the most recent amazing things I have witnessed is when He blessed us and allowed us to give food to around 500 families, tripling the size of the church overnight.

I was working outside clearing some brush one day when Victoria told me that a church member called and said we had been given some food and would be able to bless a family or two. A few hours later, they called back and said they had a twenty-foot trailer loaded with food to bring. This was unexpected and amazing. We quickly assembled a plan to go out into the community and set up to give it away the next morning.

We met at the building in which we congregate the next morning at 8:00 a.m. It began to rain. We quickly started moving the food inside. It was a huge amount; I have never seen anything like it. We took pictures and posted them to our church page and several others, letting people know it was available. We contacted other members of the church and they quickly came to help out. Soon, people started flooding in. I saw so many of the church members meeting and talking with people, inviting them to church the next day, praying with them, and also treating them as equals. This was amazing. A pickup truckload was taken to another pastor to bless another set of people, and a second truckload was taken to a community to bless even more people.

I stood there that morning afraid that we were going to waste a lot of food. I saw no earthly way that we would get all of this delivered, and we were definitely not set up to store it. But by mid-afternoon, I started worrying that we were going to run out of food. I had no more than made the statement when the phone rang and the people told us to come and get another trailer load. This was even more amazing! We went and got a second load, brought it back, and by the next afternoon, we had delivered all of that. Our attendance in church the next day had gone from around twenty-two to fifty-four! The following Sunday it was sixty-four! They kept coming. God grew His church overnight and blessed at least 500 individuals.

The food ministry was exciting. It was unexpected and had a huge impact in both the church and in many people's lives. We were excited as a church. Word was that we may be able to do this every week. As the days passed, we were calling one another asking if we had heard anything yet, about the next delivery. We were so excited to see God work and all we focused on was when would it happen again. At the last minute, we got a small load, which was wonderful, but not what we were anticipating. It then dawned on several of us that people were not coming for the food; that was merely a tool that God used to introduce them to His church. They were coming here to hear the Word of God, to be in the church. Throughout the week this was in the back of my mind. For confirmation, God showed me again on Sunday. Newcomers to the church walked up to me while I was preparing and stated, "We are not coming here for the food; we are coming for the Word." Two of them, at two different times, said the exact same thing. Message received, Lord. We will carry on and wait for the next blessing.

All too often, when God blesses us, it seems we focus on the blessing itself and yearn for more of the same. We lose sight of the big picture. That food was small change to Him; that is just a fraction of what He can do for us. We saw it as a huge blessing to not only the people, but for the growth of the church as well, so we began to get into the mindset that we needed to do this regularly. So we then started chasing the earthly source, waiting to see when this would happen next. We were met with many delays, many questions, and many periods of waiting. Things did not just magically flow and fall into place as they did the first time. Why? As we later realized, it was not God's plan for us. We were trying to chase man-made solutions and plans to make this happen; whereas the first time, it was completely unexpected and flowed like water with ease because it was God's plan, not ours. Each of us began to hear the same message: "They are not coming for the food; they are coming for the Word of God."

I recently read a passage somewhere that said people were tired of seeing different types of churches, those which were stagnant, judgmental, materialistic, exclusive, et cetera. They wanted to see a church where God was *moving*. They want to see results, and they see that here. I am a firm believer that this is because we are a Christ-led church with no dress code, no credit application, no background check, no assigned parking for those with less-than-perfect vehicles. There is no need to fill out a document giving us your debit card info on your first visit, and all of the other nonsense that some churches push today. No, I didn't imagine that or make it up to prove my point. I have actually heard people speak of these things when they tell me why they stopped going to church.

Here, we accept you as you are, just as Christ does. We break bread and enjoy fellowship together, just as Acts says. We sincerely pray over people, and we see results. We are not here to criticize you, judge you, mock you, or tell you how to live. We are here to preach and spread the Word of Jesus Christ and lead people to Him. Once people are led to Him, everything else takes care of itself. We are here for support and fellowship and to bring people to Christ, to be His hands and feet, allowing Him to do His work through us. Being obedient to His calling and instruction has led Him to bless us in many ways. That same blessing is available to you as well. We are all God's children. He respects no man, meaning that one man is not greater than the other; we are all equal in His eyes, and all of His blessings are equally available to all of us on Earth, no matter what your Earthly standing in society is; rich or poor, president of the company or janitor, sinner or saint. You just have to accept Him and let Him work in you.

On March 2020, the Living Discipleship Ministries turned one year old. In January 2020, after many people asked us to, we expanded our service. We now meet Sunday morning and evening. We started a Bible study on Wednesday evenings. We also post sermons weekly on our Facebook page. God is blessing us and His church is growing. I cannot wait to see what else He has in store. This is only the beginning.

# 8.  An Inspiring Word

T hrough all of this, I have learned many things. Life throws curves at us all the time, and the devil and his servants are prowling the Earth waiting for the opportunity to attack. Evil is a very real and present force on this Earth. The good news is that he has already been defeated by the Lamb! Therefore, with His help, you can defeat him too. People will come to attack and discourage you whether it be your choice to follow God, join in as a minister or preacher, or just follow your pursuit of happiness, career, or whatever. It is imperative that you do not let them discourage you. Stay strong in your faith, walk the walk as Christ would have you do, pray and give it to Him, and ask for His help. Do not let anger, depression, failure or stumbling blocks, or doubt get into your mind for any length of time. Once you open one of these doors, evil comes in and he is the ultimate discourager. Your head will become so filled with doubt and anger that you will never fulfill your dreams or God's plan for you. Do not allow it! Surround yourself with like-minded people of faith. These people will pray for you, encourage and support you during your endeavors. You must also reciprocate this to them. This is what Christian fellowship is all about. To uphold, encourage, and love one another as Christ loves us. Don't open the door for evil.

As I was making the decision to be obedient to what He was calling me to do—that is, to start the church and preach—I ran into many roadblocks. The main one was myself. I allowed the things of my past, my mistakes, and my temporary anger with God distract me from my true calling. One could also say that it was a training ground for God to show me what lurked behind the scenes of religion and man-made doctrine and lead me to start a part of His church as He wanted it to be, like the one in the book of Acts. There were so many pulls on me in multiple directions, and I was unsure if the avenues I was walking were God's will or a distraction. One failure on my part was the lack of prayer. You see, when in doubt, instead of trying to figure it out on your own, pray. Prayer is powerful, and once I started praying, the path was made clear.

You must also understand that not all attacks appear to be evil on the surface. The devil is cunning and deceiving. He does not always come in the form of something bad. Sometimes he appears as something innocent or good to lead you astray. Here is an example for you. For a while, every time my wife and I would start discussing the church or trying to get into Scripture, a certain someone would always either call or show up at our home. Without fail, every time, within five minutes, this person would be there. Naturally, this appeared innocent, and this person, I assume, had no idea they were interrupting our work for the Lord. They would stop to visit, need something done, et cetera.

Now, on the surface, this seems innocent enough. It seems as though this person needed help or whatever, but in reality, they were being used by the devil to distract us from Christ. We finally noticed the pattern. This person also brought arguments and anger on several occasions, and we have since cut ties with them. Before we noted the pattern, it seemed innocent. As we grew in faith and understanding, we determined otherwise. The bottom line is this: beware of anything that distracts you from Christ. Any time you sit down to study, pray, or think about your calling and you are disrupted, take note of who and what the disruption is.

One thing I learned to be true, which was told to me by others in the ministry, is that as you become closer to Christ, the evil one steps up his attack. Recognize it and defeat it with Christ! If you are feeling the call to ministry, be prepared for the attack. Use prayer for discernment, wisdom, and understanding. Do not be discouraged by the negative thoughts in your head, nor the negative words from others. If God is truly calling you, you will know it, and no one can get in His way unless you let them. Be strong in faith; if you couldn't do it, He would not have called you.

Another thing that I had to battle within myself at first was the thought, *I cannot start a church. Who am I to just start a church?* Well, I'll tell you who you are. You are the person that God has called to do this! All throughout the Bible, you see ordinary men and women being used by God to do His works. You see sinners being called, such as Saul, who became the Apostle Paul, and became a huge part of the propagation of the gospel. Are we not all sinners? Are we not all mere humans? Then why not you? You will hear those in so-called positions of authority in the "church" tell you that you are not qualified, or that you have to go to school, or that your credit score is too low to perform any ministry work. I challenge you to find any of this in the Bible. It is simply not there. The only place you will find such limiting language as this is in the man-made doctrine so often associated with "religion." Look at this Scripture:

**2 Corinthians 11:3 (KJV) But I fear, lest by any means, as the serpent beguiled Eve through his subtilty, so**

**your minds should be corrupted from the simplicity that is in Christ.**

See, the Bible even says that it is simple. Christ, although Himself is complex and the son of God, finding His love and doing His work is simple. The only rule book is the Bible. Here is a quick checklist:

1. Do you believe in God the Father Almighty and in the resurrection of his Son Jesus Christ, who died for the forgiveness of our sins?

2. Do you accept Him into your heart and have you professed with your lips that He is your Lord and Savior?

3. Have you been baptized in the name of Christ?

If you answered YES to all three, and you truly mean it from your heart, then congratulations! You are a Christian! Pretty simple, huh? Now read this:

**Matthew 28:18-20 (KJV) And Jesus came and spake unto them, saying, All power is given unto me in heaven and earth. Go ye therefore, and teach all nations, baptizing them in the name of the Father, and of the Son, and of the Holy Ghost: Teaching them to observe all things whatsoever I have commanded you: and lo, I am with you always, even unto the end of the world. Amen.**

The above Scripture is known as the Great Commission, which is our mission as Christians. Some will say that this job and authority was given only to the disciples. We will address that as well, but first I want you to see the simplicity. It says go forth to *all* nations, meaning to everyone in the world, and teach them of the gospel of Jesus Christ. It also says to baptize them in the name of the Father, the Son, and the Holy Ghost. It also says, "I am with you always!" Now, note that it did not say to have a perfect past (none of us do); it did not say go to school first; it did not say to have some human hands placed on you to give you this authority (all power is given unto Him in Heaven and Earth!); and I see no mention of a background check or requirement of a minimum credit score. You see, all that other garbage is *man-made* doctrine. It is not the requirement, nor the word of God! Simplicity!

Anyone can be called at any time. You don't just decide one day that you think working in the church is cool and that you are going to go get a degree and be a pastor. We are not building rocket ships here; you do not get to decide that. God chooses His servants, and He places the calling on their hearts that leads them to ministry. *Not* man-made rules in some religion taught at a price in some university somewhere. *No man* on Earth has the authority to place his hands on you and say you are "ordained by God." Man and education can train and certify us to be a rocket scientist, to design and build spacecraft, but the authority for ministry can only be given by God Himself.

Now, I know some folks are getting hot at me right now. I must clarify that if you went to school and received training, and have a vast knowledge of the Bible, and some piece of paper signed by a man that says you are a master theologian or whatever, good for you. You may be able to quote the Bible and know a lot of history and geography of biblical times, and that is great. It is only great, though, if you truly have the calling in your heart and you are relying on God and not the paper to do the work. I am not against education and degrees. I am against doctrine denying people who have a true calling to serve Christ strictly because of lack of earthly credentials. That requirement is not in the Bible. Do *not* let those folks discourage you from your calling. I fought that battle, and I can tell you from experience: make the jump. If God is calling you, you will not fail. He does not make mistakes.

Some have said that the Great Commission only applied to the disciples. Again, let us look at the Scripture. Jesus stated He has all authority on Heaven and Earth, so that pretty much makes Him the boss. He gives the order to go forth to teach and baptize, under His authority, so there is the command. He then says, "Teaching them to observe all things whatsoever I have commanded you:" there is your content of teaching. So here He says to teach all nations (everyone) to observe all the things I have commanded you. This means all the things He had taught them, which includes the command to teach and baptize. He then says He will be there always, even to the end of the world. Well, the disciples have long since passed, and the world is still here. So, when He said always and until the end of the world, I'm thinking that order carries on to all Christians until Jesus returns.

He says he has *all authority* in Heaven and Earth. I saw no designee anywhere that said some man on Earth could say yes or no to you carrying out an order given by Christ. I saw no place where He said you must pass this test or meet this standard, other than being a Christian, and we know how to do that. So, there you go: no man on this Earth has the authority to stop you. However, this is not a game. Study and pray on your calling, and make certain it is of God and is His will. Only you will know.

As long as we are speaking of doctrine, which adds to and takes away from the book of truth, the law, which is the Bible, and religion, which sets limitations on who and what can be done to serve God and who can do it, let me bring this Scripture to light:

> **Revelation 22:18-19 (KJV) For I testify unto every man that heareth the words of the prophecy of this book, if any man shall add unto these things, God shall add unto him the plagues that are written in this book: And if any man shall take away from the words of the book of this prophecy, God shall take away his part out of the book of life, and out of the holy city, and from the things which are written in this book.**

Again, sounds pretty straightforward and simple to me. The book is the law of God. Our instructions are clear. There is one baptism, one body (the body of Christ, the church), Christ is the head of that body, and the orders are pretty clear.

Know your Bible, know how Christ works, don't make it complicated, and remember there is only one person with authority, and He does not reside on Earth and is no longer in human form. Stand firm in the Scripture and let no man stop you from what God is calling you to do. You will meet resistance from the so-called "church" if you don't conform to their rules and doctrines. Remember this as well: it was the heads of the church and the so-called "church people" who resisted Christ and ultimately sent Him to the cross while he was on Earth. Have no fear, Christ is near (*and lo I am with you always, even to the end of the world.*)

Now that we have covered the resistance you may feel from your church or any other "church"-related entity as you move forward with your calling, we can cover some other factors from which you may feel resistance.

In my case, as I began to see God doing a work in me, I tended to write it off because I felt unworthy. We must never forget that once we have accepted Christ in our hearts, He resides within us. Therefore, we are not unworthy, as Christ is within us. We must also remember what the Scripture says in 1 John 4:4:

**1 John 4:4 (KJV) Ye are of God, little children, and have overcome them: because greater is he that is in you, than he that is in the world.**

Christ is within us and He is greater than anything you may face in the world. I can say all of these things now because I learned them during my four-year journey to the ministry. I am stronger now than I was then; at least I realize I am stronger now. Christ has always been there. I was just blind to His true power because I was raised in the "box" of religion.

I also found myself not putting enough time into reading the Bible. I was seeing many works that God was doing around me. I recognized that He was the only one who could be making things happen, but I still resisted the calling. I always caught myself saying that I was misunderstanding what I was seeing. Ultimately, I was trying to work all of this out myself and not counting on the one I needed to count on: Jesus Christ. *Prayer* is the answer. Prayer is strong and prayer works. I have seen this firsthand not only through my own prayers, but also through those around me and within the church. Prayer needs to be at the top of your list of things to do as you work through your calling. I would be faced with a challenge, a question, someone pulling me in a direction, and instead of praying about it, I would try to reason it out myself. This was a mistake and led to delays, but it was also part of God's plan. He let me see the power of prayer right when I needed to.

You must make time to follow and explore your calling. It is too easy to let work, family, friends, and just general stresses get in the way and separate you from your calling. This is part of the attack I mentioned earlier. The last thing that Satan wants is another warrior for Christ; therefore he will throw roadblocks and distractors in your path to delay you. As I said before, they don't always appear evil. It is okay to say *no* to someone. You cannot do everything for everyone all of the time—another fault of mine is my inability to use the word "no." You are embarking on a great journey, and you must make time to explore it and pray over it.

I mentioned before that my business built up two times, once before I gave in to the call and once again after the church was established. As soon as I realized and gave into my calling, my business unexpectedly crashed. Now, some would see this as depressing and begin to worry. This was a work of evil possibly trying to scare me and distract me, or perhaps God shut it down so I would devote my attention fully on Him and my calling. Only He knows that. Keep an open mind and trust in Him; keep your faith. Once the church was established, my business took off bigger than ever, right out of the blue. I knew this was a work of God and He was blessing us. However, I began to realize that I was not living up to the full potential of my calling. I was focusing more time on the business than on the ministry. Again, out of the blue, in a crazy set of circumstances, it crashed again. This time I was more in tune with what was going on. Remember that the evil one does not always come in and be immediately recognized. I saw a prospering business as a blessing, but in reality, it was a flashy distraction that made a good amount of money but took me away from the ministry. This time when it shut down,

I told Victoria that I was going to fully concentrate on the ministry and trust in the Lord to take care of us financially.

This was a bold step. The law of man tells us to work and earn a living; the law of God says to trust in Him and He will prosper you. I have found that the ministry takes most of my time and I thoroughly enjoy it. I have seen the church grow and prosper. We now have a podcast up and running, and our following on social media is growing. My family is doing well. We have a nice home, food and clothing, vehicles, and all is well. Right at the last minute, just when I begin to ask, "What are we going to do?" a financial opportunity comes through and He takes care of us. This, too, is a scary leap, but He does say to trust Him and have faith. I can attest to the fact that it does work, just as He promised.

> **Luke 9:1-3 (KJV) Then he called his twelve disciples together, and gave them power and authority over all devils, and to cure diseases. And he sent them to preach the kingdom of God, and to heal the sick. And he said unto them, Take nothing for your journey, neither staves, nor scrip, neither bread, neither money; neither have two coats apiece.**
>
> **Luke 22:35 (KJV) And he said unto them, When I sent you without purse, and scrip, and shoes, leaked ye anything? And they said, Nothing.**

Let's review the above Scriptures. He *called* His twelve disciples, gave them *power*, *sent* them to *preach* the kingdom of God. He said *take nothing*. Later, when they were doubting and questioning Him, He reminded them, "When I sent you out with nothing, did you lack anything?" The disciples replied that they *lacked nothing*. This means they were fed, clothed, and housed. They worked for the Lord, preaching the word, took nothing with them, yet did not lack anything. You have the same calling. Trust that He will take care of you. Now, this does not mean to be a lazy sluggard; when opportunities arise, you must take them—but only after careful prayer to make sure it is the will of God and not a flash in the pan from the evil one.

I have focused on my calling to be a pastor. Not all of us are called to be a pastor or to start a church. There are many types of callings into the service of the Lord. It can be through a food bank, youth ministry, music ministry, visiting with the shut-ins, as well as many other callings. I met resistance from the church I had been attending for forty years, but not everyone will meet resistance from their church. This was just the case for me and it was part of God's plan to use me in His kingdom. One thing that I see as a constant is the evil one trying to pry you from your calling. He will do anything to lead you astray. Do not fear, do not worry, instead stay focused on Christ, be in constant prayer, be open to all advice and pray over it before making any decisions.

I hope my story has been inspiring to you and that it has helped you to take confidence in your calling. I hope you will understand that no matter who says what, God is in control. No man can stop God's will. Even the devil trembles at the mention of the name Jesus Christ, yet he tells us to take comfort in that name. What a wonderful God we serve.

**LIVING DISCIPLESHIP MINISTRIES** is a church based in Chatfield, Texas, a small rural community located about an hour south of Dallas. This ministry was founded by John and Victoria Ellington with John serving as the lead pastor. We are a bible-based, non-denominational church. We base our operations off of the book of Acts and do our best to stay true to that. We promote living in discipleship, as our name states. This includes studying and learning the Scriptures to improve our walk with and knowledge of Jesus. Service above self, we strive to serve others and edify Christ as best as is humanly possible. We meet regularly, break bread together, and worship. We travel as often as we can to organize revivals and host events where we can demonstrate the love of Christ and bring as many people into the Kingdom as possible. We can be found on Facebook, where our ministry page is located. We post weekly sermons and updates on church happenings. We also have a podcast available on all major podcast platforms. We invite you to check out the church page and podcast to learn more about our ministry.

Our mailing address is PO Box 37, Chatfield, TX 75105. Feel free to send us a message on our Facebook page or email us at livingdiscipleshipministries@gmail.com.

CPSIA information can be obtained
at www.ICGtesting.com
Printed in the USA
LVHW031137261120
672640LV00007B/422

9 781633 374454